REWIRE OR RETIRE

AI for leaders: The choice that every leader must make about AI ethics, the future of work and their own leadership style to retain their edge

Marco Ryan And Alastair Lechler

Pownall
Publishing

First edition

Other books by Marco Ryan

Insider Travel Series

An Insider's 2024 Guide to Florence

An Insider's Guide to Venice

An Insider's Guide to Rome

Leadership Impact Series

The Cyber Security Blueprint for Leaders

101 Cyber Answers For Leaders

51 Essential Cyber Terms Explained For Leaders

51 Essential AI Terms Explained For Leaders

Contents

Introduction i

The Urgency of Adaptation iii
The Human Element in the AI Era iv
The Ethical Frontier iv
Rewiring for the Future v
The Path Forward vi

Chapter 1 The Digital Divide 1

The Gap of Fear 3
Rearview Mirror Leadership 4
The Unprecedented Pace of Change 5
The Organisational Handbrake 6
The Flywheel Effect 8
Bridging the Divide 10
Can you close the gap? 12
The Human Element in the AI Era 15
Moving Forward 16

Chapter 2 No Place To Hide 17

The two faces of the revolution 20
Why AI Leadership is Different 22
AI Attributes 23
Developing Digital Intelligence 28
What Remains Constant 29
The Leadership Choice 31

Chapter 3 Digital Intelligence 33

Understanding Digital Intelligence 36
The Digital Intelligence Framework 39
Measuring Your Digital Intelligence 44
Bridging the Digital Intelligence Gap 46
The Business Impact of Digital Intelligence 47
Looking Forward 49

Chapter 4 The Psychology of AI-Driven Change 51

The Fundamental Resistance Patterns 52
The Attention Deficit 56
The Resistance Loop: Five Barriers to AI Adoption 57
Decision-Making Biases Affecting AI Implementation 62
Breaking the Cycle 65
Tokio Marine Mini Case Study 68
Moving Forward 69

Chapter 5 The Ethics of AI leadership 71

Ethical Dilemmas Every Leader Must Confront 74

	The Leadership Role in Ethical Technology	78
	Going Beyond Compliance	80
	Real-World Ethical Frameworks for Non-Technical Leaders	82
	Moving Forward	84
Chapter 6	**The Sustainability Imperative**	87
	The Hidden Environmental Cost of AI	88
	AI's Dual Role	90
	The Geopolitical Wild Card	92
	The Sustainable AI Playbook	93
	What will happen in an Autonomous Future?	95
	The AI Sustainability Quadrant	97
	Moving Forward	98
Chapter 7	**The Board Dynamic**	101
	The Boardroom Expertise Gap	102
	Leading Through the Rear-View Mirror	103
	The Missing AI Governance Layer	104
	When Directors Don't Challenge Enough	106
	AI's Unique Governance Challenges	107
	The Third-Party AI Challenge	108
	Preparing for AI Crises	109
	Building the Board's AI Confidence	110
	Creating Collective AI Competence	112
	Asking the Right Questions	114
	Moving Forward	115
Chapter 8	**The C-Suite Challenge**	117
	Different Roles, Different Priorities	119
	Speed Versus Safety	123
	Different Views on Risk	125
	When Understanding Varies	127
	Moving Forward	129
Chapter 9	**The Future of Work Paradox**	131
	Beyond Simple Replacement or Augmentation	132
	Building Synthetic Teams	133
	From Passive Tools to Active Partners	133
	When Anyone Can Create Digital Solutions	134
	Curiosity Outweighs Technical Skill	135
	When Middle Management Faces Disruption	136
	Rethinking Talent in the AI Era	136
	Rapid Prototyping Becomes Essential	137
	Siemens Mini Case Study	137
	Moving Forward	139

Chapter 10 The Cultural Contradiction 143
The Adoption Fault Line 145
Winning the Talent Race 147
The Innovation-Stability Paradox 148
A Cultural Transformation Model 150
Leadership's Cultural Leverage Points 152
Moving Forward 153

Chapter 11 The Career Crossroads 155
The Vulnerability of Indecision 156
Two Paths, Both Valuable 157
The REWIRE Framework 158
The RETIRE Framework 160
Understanding Your Decision Factors 162
Making Your Decision 164
Recognising Warning Signs 168
Moving Forward 168

Chapter 12 Rewire Your Leadership Style 171
Engage 174
Widen 176
Integrate 178
Reshape 180
Evaluate 181
The Continuous Learning Loop 183

Chapter 13 Retire And Keep Involved 185
Redirect Focus 186
Empower Others 188
Translate Values 190
Influence Strategy 191
Reinforce Culture 193
Enable Transition 194
Moving Forward 195

Conclusion 197

How About A Review? 201

About the Authors 203

Leadership Impact Series 205

Resources 207

INTRODUCTION

Like the fable of the Boy calling "wolf", we have become conditioned to hearing that the latest technology is the one that will really revolutionise the world. Yet Artificial intelligence (AI) can—indeed does—have credibility in making this claim. It already impacts every facet of our lives, from content creation to medical diagnosis, predictive maintenance to the military. In workplaces worldwide, it affects our work culture, skills, and our very future. So, while many will look at the symptoms of this change and cry "technology", we have looked at some of the underlying causes and consequences, and a consistent theme emerges: Leadership.

Over the past year, we've interviewed more than 100 distinguished leaders from across the corporate, government, military and academic spectrum—from chairs of multinational corporations to owners of small businesses, from CFOs to three-star generals. What emerged is a stark picture of Leadership teams at various levels of readiness, with many of them ill-prepared, overwhelmed and in denial about the challenges and opportunities AI is bringing to the organisations they lead and to leadership in 2025 and beyond. There were exceptions, and we don't want to suggest that everything is a burning platform. We found examples of AI transformational leadership in financial services, the military, and healthcare, which indicate that many of you are already "rewiring" for the future.

Our conversations did reveal one major disconnect: many leaders are in denial about the breakneck pace of AI adoption and its far-reaching implications. This denial is not just a misjudgement. Its impact is potentially catastrophic—and we used that term advisedly.

The rise of AI agents, vibe coding, and automation is rapidly reshaping the future of work, creating both unprecedented opportunities and formidable competitive threats. These technologies are not mere tools to be delegated to the IT department; they represent a fundamental reimagining of how we conduct business, make decisions, and lead organisations.

The research reveals a further critical disconnect between the accelerating pace of AI transformation and leadership readiness. Across industries, executives acknowledge that most boardrooms or governing bodies dangerously underestimate both the speed and scale of AI disruption. This awareness gap is compounded by a fundamental lack of digital intelligence among senior leaders, particularly at the board level.

Organisations finding success with AI transformation share common approaches: they have leaders with high digital intelligence (dQ) who are digitally curious and willing to adapt; they deploy targeted proof points across business units, recognise value beyond cost-cutting, and often 'invert the pyramid' of traditional hierarchical structures to exploit the opportunities that synthetic teams and cross-functional collaboration AI demands. The most forward-thinking leaders view AI not as a mere tool but as a collaborative partner, almost like a team member with its own seat at the table.

As one executive candidly noted, "People are under-appreciating just how disruptive this is going to be... it is going to be massively disruptive, and it's going to be more disruptive for large organisations than small organisations." This reality presents leaders with a stark choice that frames our research: rewire your approach to leadership or find yourself increasingly obsolete and having to rethink your leadership relevance. There is a critical role for those who opt not to "rewire", that we have proactively called "retire", but more about that in a minute.

Perhaps the most critical insight from our research is this: AI is not a technology issue—it's a leadership imperative. The successful leaders of tomorrow will be those who deeply understand how AI, particularly generative and agentive AI, can be used strategically. They are the leaders with a high and rising dQ (Digital Intelligence), who are digitally curious. They are the leaders emboldened by lifelong learning and willing to adapt and evolve their leadership style. They are the leaders who can grasp not just the potential of the technologies but also how to manage the associated risks. Above all, they will take deliberate steps to redefine their own roles as leaders in an AI-augmented world.

The Urgency of Adaptation

The pace of AI adoption is relentless, and its impact on leadership is profound. Our research indicates that organisations with AI-savvy leaders are already pulling ahead, leveraging these technologies to make faster, better-informed decisions and to restructure their organisations into more agile and responsive teams. These leaders are not just implementing AI but reimagining their entire business models around its capabilities.

For instance, we spoke with the CEO of a global logistics company who described how AI has transformed their supply chain management. "We're not just predicting demand more accurately," he explained. "We're creating entirely new service offerings that weren't possible before. Our leadership team had to completely rethink our strategy and our role in the market."

This level of transformation requires leaders who are not just technologically literate but who possess what we call "Digital Intelligence" or dQ . This goes beyond understanding the mechanics of AI; it's about having the vision to see how these technologies can be applied to create value, solve problems, and drive innovation. Many of the traditional leadership values remain: authenticity, trust, humility, and service leadership. But with AI, these behaviours take on an increased relevance, importance, and slightly different purpose.

The Human Element in the AI Era

However, we must acknowledge a harsh truth: not everyone will be able or willing to "rewire" themselves for this new reality. For those who choose not to adapt, there is a vital role to play in the next five years. This isn't the traditional retirement path of a gold watch, more time with the grandkids or indulging in your favourite hobby; it's an opportunity to redefine their role into a Mentor, Coach and "Human conscience". Their role becomes one of stewardship—to guide the next generation of leaders, imparting the irreplaceable human elements of leadership that AI cannot replicate.

A former board chair of a Fortune 500 company put it eloquently: "AI can crunch numbers and spot patterns, but it can't inspire a team or navigate the nuances of corporate politics. There's still an enormous need for human wisdom and experience."

This was a theme that kept reappearing across our interviews. While AI is transforming who will lead, it's also highlighting the irreplaceable qualities of human leaders: empathy, ethical judgment, and the ability to navigate complex social and emotional situations. The "human-in-the-loop" is fast becoming an important component of effective AI systems. However, it requires skills such as prompt engineering to be able to interface and use AI correctly. Even if a leader is not fully AI literate, those unable to interface with, work alongside, interrogate or prompt AI tools will be disadvantaged.

The Ethical Frontier

Leaders face new ethical challenges as AI becomes more prevalent in decision-making processes. How do we ensure that AI systems are fair and unbiased? How do we maintain transparency and accountability when algorithms increasingly make decisions? As one of the generals we interviewed put it: "You need to be able to look at yourself in the mirror. Ethics is not something you can delegate."

These questions are not just theoretical; they have real-world implications. A tech executive we interviewed shared a cautionary tale: "We implemented an AI system for employee performance evaluations, only to discover it was perpetuating gender biases. It was a wake-up call. We realised that ethical oversight of AI isn't just a nice-to-have; it's a critical leadership function."

Leaders must now become stewards of ethical AI use, ensuring that these powerful tools are deployed responsibly and aligned with organisational values and societal norms.

Rewiring for the Future

Our research reveals that truly effective AI leadership requires nothing short of a neural rewiring—a fundamental reconfiguration of how executives think, decide, and lead. This isn't merely adopting new skills or technologies; it demands a comprehensive reimagining of leadership itself. The leaders who thrive in this new landscape are those who develop an intimate understanding of AI's capabilities while maintaining the uniquely human wisdom to discern when technology should take precedence and when human judgment remains irreplaceable. They cultivate organisational cultures where experimentation flourishes, where failure becomes a valued teacher, and where traditional hierarchies dissolve in favour of fluid, responsive structures built around AI-augmented workflows. It required boldness yet humility; it requires fast decision making, yet being open to the 'wisdom of crowds'. It requires confidence, transparency and at times vulnerability. What is clear is that there is little or no place to hide.

Perhaps most challenging of all, this rewiring process forces leaders to confront deeply ingrained mental models about authority, expertise, and control. Those who succeed don't simply delegate AI initiatives to technical teams; they immerse themselves in understanding how these technologies transform core business assumptions. They balance data-driven insights with intuitive understanding, recognising that leadership in the AI age requires both algorithmic literacy and profound human connection. The stark reality is that leaders who cannot—or will not—undertake this neurological rewiring will increasingly find themselves unable to navigate the rapidly transforming business landscape, regardless of their past successes or current position.

Whether through ego, through a lack of understanding about the true pace of change, or an over-reliance on what we described as "rear-view mirror thinking", some leaders do not dare to step aside. But part of being a great leader is recognising when your time is up = when you need to make way for emerging talent, different skills, or a different style. All too often, and to the organisation's detriment, Leaders stay on too long. Part of the rationale for this book is to face that challenge. To ask yourself the hard questions.

One CEO described her rewiring journey: "I had to unlearn many of the leadership practices I'd relied on for decades. It was uncomfortable, even scary, at times. But it was also exhilarating. I feel like I'm leading in a whole new way now, with AI as a powerful ally."

Whether agility will trump ability is yet to be tested; one thing that differs with AI is the incredible pace with which it unfolds. One of the reasons we went down a self-published route was that, despite offers from traditional publishers to discuss the book, their publishing model meant there was a six to eight-month publishing process we had to follow. We were worried that we would be out of date before publishing! This pace means that leaders everywhere will be tested in their ability to pivot organisations quickly or to change ways of working or processes at a pace that has hitherto been unknown.

The Path Forward

In this book, we delve deep into these themes, exploring the realities of the AI revolution, the psychological and ethical challenges it presents, and the strategies for personal and organisational transformation. We examine the changing dynamics within C-suites and boardrooms and offer frameworks for both "rewiring" and "retiring" with purpose.

Those frameworks are built around the words REWIRE and RETIRE, using them both as mnemonics to help frame a pathway that leaders can take tangible actions to develop their careers. Whilst the title was deliberately designed to raise a wry smile, we believe there is an enormous value in having leaders actively working in either the rewire or retire mindsets. The danger is when inertia or indecision means that a leader has not chosen.

Our goal is not to prophesy doom or promise utopia. Instead, we aim to provide a clear-eyed, practical guide for the AI-driven future of leadership. Whether you're a seasoned executive or an aspiring leader, this book will equip you with the insights and strategies needed to thrive in the age of AI.

We had wanted to begin each chapter with an engaging and narrative story—proof of AI in action or an exemplar of best practice to make it engaging and to provide reassurance that what followed in the chapter was possible for anyone. Sadly, the recency of AI, the speed at which it has enveloped us, has also translated into a dearth of completed use cases. Many of the executives we spoke to had compelling stories to tell, but those stories were often too early-stage or still being written. Indeed, the vast majority of our interviews were conducted on the basis that we would not name companies or individuals, as what we were discussing was very much a "work in progress". There was definitely a degree of apprehension about talking publicly about something that was not complete, published or "signed off"

We are hugely grateful to all those individuals for the time they gave us, for the generosity of their insight, the honesty of their learning, and the encouragement we received. To those who were able to go on the record, you will see them referenced in the following chapters, and we are grateful for their leadership and their willingness to participate in this project publicly.

Although the changes that AI is heralding are exciting and overwhelming with equal measure, one thing is sure: the leaders who embrace AI will be the ones who shape the future. They will be the ones who create organisations that are not just more efficient but more human, leveraging technology to free up time for creativity, innovation, and meaningful human connections.

The journey ahead is challenging, but it's also filled with unprecedented opportunities. It requires courage, vision, and a willingness to embrace change. But the rewards are immense for those willing to leap. You have the chance to be at the forefront of a leadership revolution, shape the future of work, and create more adaptive, innovative, and impactful organisations than ever before.

As Andrew Ng, the Former Chief Scientist at Baidu Research, put it, "Five years from now, there will be a number of S&P 500 CEOs who will wish they'd started thinking earlier about their AI strategy." We hope that, partly because of this book, you will not be one of them!

The choice before us as leaders is clear: rewire or retire. The following pages will help you make that decision confidently and chart a course for success, whatever path you choose. The future of leadership is being written now, and with this book, we invite you to be its author.

The future of leadership is here. Are you ready to rewire?

Chapter 1
THE DIGITAL DIVIDE

In the rolling hills of California wine country, a family-owned winery with a forty-year heritage faced an uncomfortable truth. Despite their reputation for exceptional wines, they were facing an existential threat. The wine market was shrinking, and consumer preferences were shifting toward alternatives—alcoholic seltzers, cannabis products, and other modern choices. Meanwhile, the winery was still managing its business through Excel spreadsheets, much as it had done since the 1980s. They were not alone.

Only about 5% of winemakers in California are actually profitable—and they were one of them—and so the winery realised they had to do something dramatic to adapt and grow in the rapidly changing world. Their response was bold. Where many leaders might have pursued incremental improvements or limited experiments, the winery recognised both the depth of the market shift and what would be required to adapt to it.

"They realised they had a massive problem," explains Nick Milne-Home, President of Computomic, whose company was brought in to consult on the digital transformation. "And they felt that the only way to solve it was through data, specifically a profound understanding of their customer and market data."

The consultation led to a series of discussions (almost educational sessions) and finally a recommendation for an enterprise-grade data lake solution—technology that might seem excessive for a vineyard operation, yet one that provides it with the ability to leapfrog into an AI-led world.

"Implementing a modern data platform will solve your problem, but it's potentially overkill," explained Milne-Home to the winery owner. The response from the owner was telling. "We understand, but we've got to get this right, and have to do it now. '"

This clarity of purpose drove a comprehensive transformation. Rather than isolating the changes to one department or system, the winery rebuilt its entire operational infrastructure—CRM, ordering, marketing, and finance systems all transitioned to create a unified data environment capable of supporting AI-driven decision-making.

For a traditional agricultural business, this transformed how the owners thought about their role and how they created value. Farmers who had spent generations perfecting their understanding of soil, climate, and grape varieties were now equally focused on understanding customer data, market patterns, and AI predictive allocation models.

"They've realised that the success of their business actually rests on data and AI," Milne-Home observed. "And without that, they may not survive."

In an industry where heritage and tradition are powerful forces, this owner chose to embrace unfamiliar technology that promised to secure the next century of the winery's future rather than protect the comfortable patterns of the past. The owner had seen, embraced and crossed the 'Digital Divide'.

The Gap of Fear

The Digital Divide—a term that originally described inequalities in internet access—now represents something far more consequential: a rapidly widening performance gap between organisations that can use AI and digital, and those that cannot.

On the far side stand digital 'pureplay' companies, with enviable valuations, a culture of innovation and agility, bursting with digital natives and AI woven into their DNA. On the nearside, stand traditional companies, hamstrung by legacy systems, outdated mindsets, creaking operating models, and what we've come to call "rearview mirror leadership". And the gap is widening at a pace that few have ever experienced.

There are several reasons that organisations struggle to cross the divide, and we will examine each in more detail in a minute, but we grouped them into four main groups: pace, the organisational handbrake, the flywheel effect and leadership. In our research and in talking to over a hundred leaders in large companies, government departments, the military, non-profit organisations, successful medium-sized companies, investors, and strategists, the most significant factor of those four was leadership behaviour.

Many of the leaders we talked to felt overwhelmed by their lack of understanding, the technology and AI choices available, and their fear of "getting it wrong on their watch".

Many mentioned the fear of looking incompetent ("I don't know what I don't know"), the fear stemming from a lack of technical knowledge ("I just don't understand this stuff"), and fear disguised as time poverty ("I just don't have the time"). Fear becomes a psychological barrier that shows up in both leadership and organisational behaviour. You probably recognise them: analysis paralysis, incremental approaches, and proof-of-concept purgatory.

"The fear of messing up is still way stronger than the fear of missing out ... Fear is absolutely holding leaders back, and the need for success isn't sufficiently visible to overcome the fear yet," explains Nick Milne-Home, who has helped hundreds of companies address this exact challenge.

Overcoming those fears is much of what this book will dive into in great detail, providing simplified explanations, case studies, encouragement and insight into how leaders can break that cycle of fear and begin to rewire.

For many, fear remains a very real reaction to the leadership challenge. That can create a deeply rooted inertia in Leadership behaviours and reinforce the need to look backwards to what they know and understand, rather than forward to a world of risk and uncertainty.

Rearview Mirror Leadership

Imagine driving a car using only the rearview mirror. Absurd, yet this is how many executives lead digital transformation. They make decisions based on past performance and established metrics while cautiously experimenting with innovation without fully committing.

For many leaders, this backwards focus feels more comfortable. The past is known and quantifiable, the foundation of their decades of success. The future, transformed by AI, demands new skills and creates uncertainty.

Mikko Tepponen, COO and CDO at FLSmidth, observes: "These multinationals or established industrial companies like ours are about 150 years old. They've been around the block and are firmly established in a known market. But that longevity, once an unquestionable asset, now sometimes functions as an anchor rather than a sail."

The danger lies in how invisible this rearview leadership is. Most executives don't recognise they're doing it. They believe they're forward-thinking because they've approved an "AI strategy" or hired a Chief Digital Officer, but these actions often mask a deeper unwillingness to rethink operations fundamentally.

Nick Milne-Home explains: "You've got to recognise that you've got a problem before you can even start to solve it. And you've got to be open-minded if you want to solve it in a comprehensive way. The challenge for most business leaders is that they really struggle to recognise they've got a problem... and even if they do get their heads around it, they put it on the all too difficult pile."

True forward-looking leadership demands reimagining your entire business through a digital lens. Marianne Culver, a Non-Executive director of a PE Company and a FTSE 250 industrial company, describes this mindset shift: "Digital is more of an attitude starting with the leadership teams than some kind of transactional technical project. It's about future innovation, creativity, and harnessing the power of data... and how comfortable leaders are with future-forward thinking."

Business leadership is undergoing dramatic change—arguably a seismic shift or a once-in-a-lifetime moment. Tomorrow's leaders will be those standing on the far bank of the digital divide—those who anticipate technological disruption, pivot strategies mid-flight, and create cultures where innovation is embedded in the organisational DNA.

The consequences for leaders failing to adapt are increasingly severe. Once-dominant companies falter, outpaced by more digitally capable competitors who recognised earlier that technology is the foundation of business strategy. Disrupt or be disrupted.

One key quality of great leaders is stewardship—leaving the organisation in a better state than when you took over. With AI's existential challenge, leaders must "rewire" how they lead or step aside. As Nick Milne-Home puts it: "What's not okay is to dig your heels in and say, 'Well, I've only got five years left to push as CFO and hang the rest of them, because that's my pension plan.' You've got to find a new course".

The Unprecedented Pace of Change

The sheer velocity of AI change has caught even the most vigilant leaders off guard, widening the digital divide. Our research revealed four distinct leadership responses: the sceptics in denial, the aware but overwhelmed, the engaged but resource-constrained, and the fully involved but perhaps naïve about scaling requirements. Most of us fit into one of these categories, and apart from the sceptics, we're all keenly aware of AI's exponential pace.

"About six to eight months ago, I could see the shift happening and the rapid pace of change in AI. A new model or tool seems to be coming out each day, and it moves everything at a hundred times," observes Graham Donoghue, CEO of Forge Holidays. "I never want to get left behind."

This isn't gradual evolution—it's revolution, and the window for adaptation narrows daily. What once took years now takes weeks. When one of the authors was the Chief Digital Officer at Wärtsilä in 2017, his team built a state-of-the-art micro-learning app for 17,000 employees. It required nine months, a team of ten and nearly one million dollars. Recently, using two 'vibe coding' apps (Apps that allow you to use prompts to configure full technology solutions) costing just £40 per month each, he recreated the entire project—front-end design, gamification, full stack deployment, and AI automation—in two days.

This acceleration isn't merely technological—it creates new business models, shifts consumer expectations, and redefines competitive landscapes overnight. A mid-sized retailer's CFO shared a sobering reality check: "We thought we had time to catch up. We were wrong. In just 18 months, we lost 20% of our market share to a startup that offered a seamless digital experience."

This is the cruel mathematics of exponential change: by the time many leaders recognise the threat, they're already months or years behind. The democratisation of AI through tools like ChatGPT has intensified this dynamic. Leaders who invest in the capabilities to exploit this shift will anticipate market changes, optimise operations, and create better solutions for their customers at scale.

Most organisations simply aren't where they need to be. The consequences are already evident: market share losses, decreased productivity, and talent drain to more digitally savvy competitors.

The Organisational Handbrake

Even when leaders intellectually grasp the AI imperative, they often struggle to drive meaningful change. The issue isn't awareness—it's execution.

Our interviews revealed a consistent pattern we call "the organisational handbrake"—a blend of cultural, structural, and mindset barriers that prevent established companies from moving at the speed AI demands.

Traditional hierarchies can suffocate innovation before it has a chance to breathe. While digital natives make decisions in hours, established organisations force AI initiatives through approval labyrinths where momentum withers. Each additional signature multiplies the chance that transformative ideas will be diluted beyond recognition.

Risk aversion masquerades as prudence but functions as paralysis. In boardrooms worldwide, executives demand breakthrough thinking while recoiling from the experiments and inevitable missteps that produce it. This creates a culture where mediocrity becomes the safest career strategy.

The resistance often shows up as generational tension. Nick Milne-Home observed this dynamic playing out across organisations: "We see baby boomers and Gen X, particularly in the IT field, throwing up every technical obstacle possible. They undermine change in every possible way because they're terrified of losing their jobs. Meanwhile, millennials, Gen Y and others are like, 'What are we doing with IT? Why can't we just do it? I don't need IT, I can just do it on my phone'."

This tension can lead to extreme responses. In the US, the new Department of Government Efficiency (DOGE), under Elon Musk, is forcing radical change. While we're not making a political point or endorsing the approach, it represents a fascinating case study in demolishing organisational handbrakes. As Milne-Home describes it: "You've got a couple of hundred tech experts in their twenties blowing up everything, and they're just going in. And they're saying, 'Just go. We don't need you and your old IT, who gives a damn about the past and how you've always done it, it doesn't matter.'" This slash-and-burn method creates its own problems, but it does illuminate the frustration with institutional inertia.

The result? AI initiatives become isolated projects rather than transformative forces. Initial experiments, constrained by organisational limitations, deliver underwhelming results, which then "prove" that AI isn't worth the investment, further limiting commitment.

What makes this challenge particularly thorny is that it's not a technology issue at all—it's fundamentally about leadership. The gap between organisations continues to widen as early adopters deploy sophisticated AI tools while others face an increasingly steep climb to relevance.

Breaking this cycle requires the courage to dismantle longstanding practices and create space for genuine reinvention. Leaders must recognise that AI-powered digital transformation is like previous digital transformation but on steroids. AI-led change isn't a one-time project but a continuous journey, with emerging technologies as its driving force, and leadership agility as a core competence. In this type of transformation, there are no manual handbrakes.

The Flywheel Effect

Over the past twenty-five years, we've witnessed the rise of "pure play" digital companies—organisations born in the cloud, operating with a digital-first mentality, and built on modern, adaptive technology stacks. These enterprises, from tech giants like Google to thousands of digital-native startups, offer crucial lessons for traditional companies struggling with transformation.

Their advantage stems from what we call "the flywheel effect"—five interconnected disciplines or gears that, when properly meshed, create accelerating momentum. The gears can be different sizes or swapped out to change the "gearing ratio," but they must still mesh together.

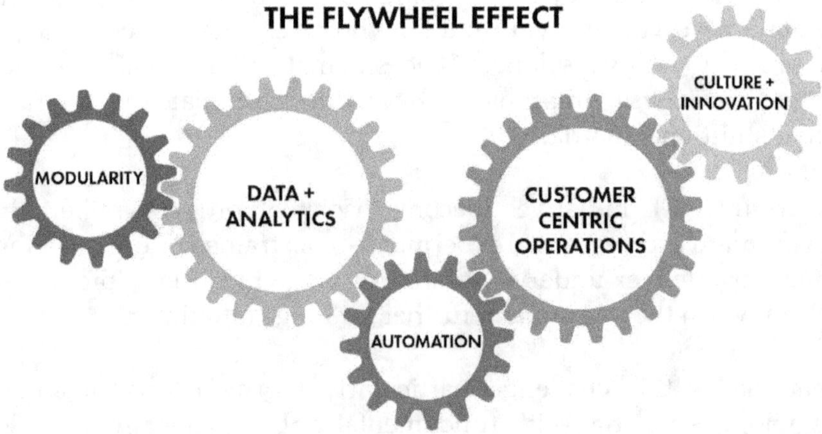

The five main gears in this flywheel are:

- ***Customer-centric operations*** that continuously evolve based on a deep understanding of user needs, with AI-powered personalisation at scale. These operations understand customer needs, build products that directly address those needs, and refine them using feedback and behavioural data. Increasingly, data collection, analysis, and action can be automated, and AI can be used to drive hyper-personalisation at scale.

- ***Data analytics and AI-enhanced algorithms*** are driving decision-making at all organisational levels. This creates a culture where data-driven decision-making permeates every aspect of operations.

- ***Modularity.*** Platform-based business models built on a modular architecture can scale rapidly and create network effects. This starts with microservices, but modularity can extend to features, applications, or whole business models that can be "plug-and-played" into broader ecosystems or with partners.

- ***A culture of innovation*** embraces continuous experimentation, where failure is reframed as learning. The tools, ways of working, and culture become entirely digital, fostering adaptability and constant evolution.

- ***Automation,*** from edge processing to agentic AI, reduces costs while increasing speed and capabilities. This ranges from IoT edge processing and gathering data at scale to Agentic AI, RPA, and other ways to automate processes, reduce costs, and increase pace.

For a truly digitally enabled organisation, these elements aren't separate initiatives—they're a unified operating system. Their advantage isn't merely technological; it's organisational. They don't have to transform—they were born transformed.

The contrast with traditional organisations couldn't be starker. Where pure plays build seamless digital experiences from the ground up, established companies struggle to integrate new capabilities with legacy systems. Where digital organisations make data-driven decisions by default, traditional organisations battle siloed information and disconnected systems. It is not enough to have some of the gears. All are required to create the flywheel effect.

Nick Milne-Home again: "If you don't understand those gears, and if you don't embrace them, you will die. It's not a question of 'if', just 'when'."

The rise of fintech companies in the banking sector illustrates this phenomenon perfectly. These agile startups have disrupted traditional banking models by offering frictionless digital experiences, personalised services, and innovative financial products. They have built tightly coupled solutions, driven by great data and customer insight, on platforms designed to scale and allow them to partner and be "modular". Their success has forced established banks to reevaluate their entire approach to customer service and product development.

A board member of a global bank reflected on this shift: "We used to think our size and history were our greatest assets. Now we realise they can be liabilities if we don't learn to move with the speed of our digital-native competitors who are personalising every customer interaction" (Taylor, 2024).

Bridging the Divide

Closing the digital divide isn't primarily a technology problem—it's a leadership challenge. Our research has identified six critical capabilities leaders must develop to navigate the AI revolution:

Digital Intelligence (dQ)

Developing a working understanding of AI capabilities and limitations—not to become technical experts, but to make informed strategic decisions. This goes beyond surface-level knowledge to a proper comprehension of how these technologies can drive value and innovation. Leaders must cultivate a deep understanding of emerging technologies and their business implications.

Adaptive Learning

Creating organisational environments where experimentation is encouraged and failure is treated as valuable feedback. This requires a shift from traditional hierarchical structures to more flexible, team-based approaches. Organisations must foster a culture of continuous learning and establish formal programmes to upskill employees at all levels on digital technologies.

Data Fluency

Building the ability to interpret and act on data insights, balancing analytical inputs with human judgment. Leaders must learn to leverage data analytics to inform strategic decisions. This requires not just investing in data infrastructure but also developing the skills to interpret and act on data insights.

Talent Magnetism

Attracting and retaining digitally skilled professionals by creating environments where they can thrive. This often requires rethinking traditional HR practices and creating a work environment that appeals to tech-savvy professionals. Companies should consider creating hybrid roles that combine domain expertise with technical skills.

Ecosystem Thinking

Breaking down silos and fostering collaboration across functions, partners, and even competitors. Digital transformation requires collaboration between business, specialists, and IT teams. Cross-functional teams should be empowered to solve business problems using digital tools.

Digital Curiosity

AI can be liberating. It can free us from daily manual tasks that have little value and create space for digital curiosity to explore and ask, "What if?" This mindset embraces things like Vibe coding to quickly spin up a Minimal Viable Product (MVP) in hours, allowing ideas to come to life and be tested in very short order. It is a mix of creativity, innovation, and boldness, and it requires leaders to constantly seek to understand new developments, to loop back, and to ask: "Can we solve this now, given that this technology is now available?"

These capabilities don't develop overnight. They require intentional focus and consistent practice. As one CEO we talked with, who had successfully led her organisation through digital transformation, shared: "We realised that technology wasn't the main barrier—it was our own mindset. We had to learn to think differently, to challenge our assumptions, and to be comfortable with constant change. Our biggest breakthrough came when we stopped viewing digital as a technical initiative and started seeing it as a business transformation enabled by technology. It wasn't easy, but it was necessary for our survival".

The stakes couldn't be higher. Organisations that fail to bridge the divide face a triple threat that can quickly become terminal: market irrelevance as digitally savvy competitors seize market share at breathtaking speed; margin compression as AI-enabled rivals operate with fundamentally lower cost structures; and talent exodus as your best minds flee to environments where their skills won't wither on the vine.

This isn't abstract business theory—it's the brutal reality of reshaping industry after industry. The tombstones of corporate history tell the same story: Blockbuster paralysed while Netflix innovated, Borders remained static while Amazon evolved, and traditional taxis protested while Uber expanded. The message is unmistakable: transform or become a cautionary tale in someone else's business school case study.

"The companies that pull ahead in the coming years won't necessarily be those with the most advanced technology," notes Charlene Li, a leading digital transformation consultant. "They'll be the ones whose leaders can envision how these technologies can solve real business problems and who can mobilise their organisations to execute on that vision" (Li, 2024).

Can you close the gap?

The easy answer is: "Yes." The slightly more truthful answer is "yes, but..." And the "but" is really about the leadership intent. We have emphasised that AI success is not about the technology, but about leadership, because we are emphasising that this is all about a change in strategy, operating model and the ways of working. Those are all leadership issues. But if our Winegrowers in California have not yet convinced you, here are two large multinationals, in very different sectors, that have affected a similar transformation. It is often harder to stop and turn the tanker than the speedboat, but these case studies should provide some insight into the reality that this is possible.

DBS—A mini case study

DBS Bank of Singapore transformed itself from a traditional financial institution into "a technology company with a banking license," reimagining its entire business model and organisational culture with digital capabilities at the core.

When DBS's board gathered in 2013, they reached a conclusion that would fundamentally reshape the company's future. As CEO, Piyush Gupta recalls, "We felt that if we didn't lead the charge, frankly, we might die". This wasn't hyperbole—it was recognition that banking was perhaps "the most digitisable industry of all."

What distinguished DBS's approach was their refusal to apply what Gupta calls "digital lipstick." Instead, they committed to three transformative priorities: completely digitising operations, embedding themselves in the customer journey, and creating a culture that could compete with businesses "that work out of a garage, take risks, operate in a nimble way."

Rather than creating a separate innovation unit, DBS "attacked the core" of the organisation. They built technology literacy through hackathons where employees partnered with startups to build working apps in 72 hours. By 2015, experimentation had become mandatory—every employee ran an experiment, resulting in 1,000 experiments across the bank.

"If you want to make change real, and if you really want to make change cohesive, then you have to attack the core," Gupta explains. Physical spaces were redesigned with the help of anthropologists, creating open environments where people "stand up, conduct 'agile' meetings, do post-its on the walls, and huddle together in scrums every morning."

The results speak volumes: call-centre headcount reduced from 700 to under 500 despite higher volumes; ATM management improvements saved SGD 20 million; cross-border remittances increased five-fold, generating SGD 75 million in new revenue; bank assurance market share doubled to 35%.

Their mobile-only bank in India—"completely paperless and branchless"—gained 800,000 customers in just nine months, operating with only 25% of traditional staffing.

None of this would have been possible without board-level courage. Directors allocated an additional SGD 200 million to, in their words, "go blow it up." This created the space for DBS to answer Gupta's rallying question: "How do you create a 22,000-person start-up?"

RIO Tinto: A mini case study

Similarly, Rio Tinto highlights that leadership intent can transform even the most established players in traditionally physical industries.

For many, mining evokes bulldozers and dust, not data scientists and algorithms. Yet Rio Tinto, a 150-year-old mining company, has transformed itself into an AI-powered operation that rivals tech natives in its sophistication.

Seven years ago, while peers were still debating whether AI might someday be relevant, Rio Tinto's leadership established a dedicated machine learning team to work across their global operations—from aluminium in Brisbane to iron ore in Perth.

Rather than creating isolated digital experiments—the typical corporate response—they recognised that crossing the digital divide required fundamental changes to their operating model.

"We wanted to make Machine Learning (ML) development accessible and scalable across the entire organisation," explained their digital transformation lead. This translated into creating centralised MLOps capabilities that automated deployment workflows and security processes.

The results are telling. Today, predictive maintenance models provide a seven-week advance notice for rail maintenance, avoiding costly disruptions. In Canadian smelters, ML models predict water leaks that could lead to dangerous hydrogen gas buildup, significantly reducing safety risks.

The company democratised AI throughout the organisation with platforms that allowed non-technical "citizen data users" to build models without specialised coding knowledge. This wasn't just about technology—it was about fundamentally changing how people worked.

The journey wasn't without challenges. They had to navigate complex issues around data accessibility across multiple air-gapped data lakes while balancing security protocols with innovation needs.

Rio Tinto excelled in the leadership's willingness to tackle structural challenges head-on rather than letting them become excuses for inaction.

The Human Element in the AI Era

We must acknowledge a hard truth: not everyone will be able or willing to "rewire" themselves for this new reality. For those who choose not to adapt, there is still a vital role to play in the next five years—it's an opportunity to mentor and guide the next generation of leaders, imparting the irreplaceable human elements of leadership that AI cannot replicate.

A former board chair of a Fortune 500 company put it eloquently: "AI can crunch numbers and spot patterns, but it can't inspire a team or navigate the nuances of corporate politics. There's still an enormous need for human wisdom and experience".

This sentiment was echoed across many of our interviews. While AI is transforming leadership, it's also highlighting the imperative nature of human-centred AI transformation.

The concept of "rewiring" emerged as a central theme in our research. It's not just about learning new skills; it's about fundamentally altering one's approach to leadership, leaning harder into some well-established leadership qualities, casting off outdated approaches, and adopting new skills. This rewiring process involves developing a deep understanding of AI capabilities and limitations, cultivating a mindset of continuous learning and adaptation, fostering a culture of innovation and experimentation, balancing data-driven decision-making with human intuition and wisdom, and reimagining organisational structures and processes to leverage AI effectively.

Moving Forward

The digital divide represents more than a technological gap—it reflects a fundamental leadership challenge. As we've seen throughout this chapter, organisations that successfully overcome this divide share a common trait: leadership that understands the strategic implications of digital technologies and can drive transformation throughout their organisations.

The lessons from companies like Rio Tinto and DBS Bank demonstrate that digital leadership is possible in any industry, regardless of its traditional nature. What matters is not the industry itself but the vision and commitment of its leaders.

The situation is clear: with AI, we are not witnessing a passing technology trend but a seismic force that is challenging the very nature of what organisations are and how we do business.

The divide is real, and it's widening. The consequences of falling behind are becoming more severe by the day.

But in case you think that this is all rather "doom and gloom", we view this as an enormous and positive opportunity. While it is undoubtedly a leadership challenge, it is one that, with some focus, some structured thinking, some increased process prioritisation, and proper time commitment, is well worth tackling.

The rewards for the organisation, its commercial success, your colleagues' future, and, just as importantly, personally for you are enormous. It is arguably one of the most exciting times to be a leader, with so much unwritten and so much to play for.

Chapter 2

NO PLACE TO HIDE

Lieutenant General Sir Tom Copinger-Symes faced a critical decision. His team was attempting something radical: a "moonshot" project based on radically different ideas, thinking, and data that could transform how the UK Armed Forces measured and modelled their readiness for deployment. Part of that included the unthinkable action of deploying sensitive military data to the cloud—a move that contradicted established security protocols but could unlock breakthrough capabilities for British defence. Traditional risk assessment methods offered little guidance in this unfamiliar territory.

"I'd spent years…dealing with risk in all forms," he recalls. "But suddenly, I was in a new digital environment, where my experience was light, my risk appetite untested …and where I can see the value, but others can't see it."

The turning point came when a trusted security architect challenged him: "Sir, I think it is fair to say that I know more about security architecture than you ever will. If we have to wait until you get 80% of your mind comfortable around the security [risk], it will be too slow. According to the architecture that I see, this [the cloud] is technically safer than anywhere else we could put it, including our own systems, even if nobody believes it. Are you prepared to accept that risk, and trust me?"

Copinger-Symes made the call: "Let's get on and do it."

This moment captures the essence of leadership in the AI era. The fundamental principles—clarity of purpose, considered risk-taking, decisive action—remain constant. However, the context in which these principles operate has transformed dramatically. Leaders must now make consequential decisions with less certainty, draw on expertise they don't personally possess, and accept risks they can't fully quantify.

"It's not about the technology," Copinger-Symes emphasises. "It's about what the technology allows us to do and how we can defend the nation better with technology... but it's really that leadership is different in this digital age."

This ability to lead in the fog of the "AI war" is a challenge that is not unique to the military. Leaders from manufacturing to finance, healthcare to retail, are confronting the same reality: artificial intelligence has moved beyond merely another technology trend to become a fundamental shift in leadership and strategy that is reshaping how organisations operate and how leadership works.

At Citibank, executives found themselves rewriting risk management frameworks when AI credit algorithms began identifying qualified borrowers who would have been rejected under traditional models. In manufacturing, Toyota plant managers had to reconsider operational control when AI systems began suggesting production line configurations that contradicted decades of established practice but delivered superior results.

"This is the biggest technological change of my lifetime. It is up there with the creation of the Internet. It's a game changer," notes Simon Lucas, CEO of Society, an executive leadership search firm. His sentiment captures what many leaders are experiencing—a sense that the ground is shifting beneath their feet.

Leadership capabilities that were once optional luxuries—comfort with ambiguity, willingness to challenge convention, openness to expertise regardless of hierarchy—have become essential survival traits.

AI's Rapid Evolution: What You Need to Know

Before we dive deeper into the impact of AI on leadership, we need to take a brief step back to ensure that we have a shared understanding of what AI is and how we have got to the position we find ourselves in today.

The concept of artificial intelligence emerged in the 1950s through the pioneering work of Alan Turing and John McCarthy. For decades, progress came in fits and starts—periods of breakthrough excitement followed by "AI winters" when funding dried up amid disappointed expectations. Much of this really had to do with the technological limitation of machines; the processors simply weren't powerful enough.

A critical inflection point occurred around the turn of the century. The digital explosion generated vast quantities of data while computing power grew exponentially cheaper, following Moore's Law. Machine learning—a technique allowing systems to improve through experience rather than explicit programming—suddenly became practical at scale. Researchers have developed increasingly sophisticated algorithms capable of discovering patterns in data that are too complex for humans to perceive.

The 2010s brought breakthrough advances in deep learning, a subset of machine learning using neural networks with multiple layers. In 2012, during the ImageNet competition (a benchmark for computer vision), a neural network called AlexNet dramatically outperformed its traditional rivals. Combined with some dramatic new processor architectures and capabilities, it acted as a watershed moment, generating renewed interest and investment in AI. Companies like Google, Facebook, and Microsoft began pouring billions into research and development.

Then came 2023, a year that fundamentally altered public perception of AI's capabilities. When OpenAI released ChatGPT to the public, something remarkable occurred. Millions experienced sophisticated AI firsthand for the first time, generating essays, code, poetry, and business plans with apparent understanding and creativity. As Stanford professor Fei-Fei Li observed, we reached an "inflection moment" where public awareness finally caught up with what had been happening in research labs for years.

The two faces of the revolution

When leaders discuss "AI," they're actually referring to a family of technologies rather than a single tool. At its most basic level, we have traditional rules-based systems—software that follows explicit instructions set by humans, like the fraud detection systems that flag unusual credit card transactions based on predetermined rules about spending patterns.

Then came machine learning, where systems learn patterns from data without being explicitly programmed. These systems improve through experience, much like the recommendation engines that power Netflix suggestions or the predictive maintenance software that tells factory managers when equipment needs attention before it fails.

More recently, we've seen the emergence of deep learning, which uses neural networks inspired by the human brain to tackle increasingly complex problems. These systems can identify subtle patterns in vast datasets that would be impossible for humans to spot—think of how medical imaging AI can detect early signs of disease that even experienced radiologists might miss. It's within this deep learning branch that both generative AI and agentic AI have emerged as powerful applications.

Generative AI represents a significant leap in deep learning capabilities, trained on massive datasets to create new content rather than simply analyse existing information. When a marketing team uses AI to draft product descriptions in multiple languages or when designers use it to create variations of packaging designs, they're harnessing generative AI to amplify their creative process.

Meanwhile, agentic AI takes these capabilities a step further by adding decision-making autonomy—moving from systems that respond to our prompts to systems that act independently within defined parameters. When autonomous supply chain systems reroute deliveries during unexpected weather events without human intervention, or when smart building systems adjust energy usage based on occupancy patterns, they're demonstrating the independent action that defines agentic AI. Think of them as cousins in the AI family tree: generative AI creates when asked, while agentic AI decides and acts on its own.

Understanding these distinctions helps make sense of how each is reshaping different aspects of organisational leadership in ways that go far beyond mere efficiency gains.

Generative AI

It produces text, images, music, code, and more based on prompts. These systems analyse massive datasets to identify patterns, then generate original outputs that often appear remarkably human-like. Using ChatGPT to draft an email or DALL-E to create an image means engaging with generative AI.

The underlying technology, known as transformer models, represents a fundamental advance in machine learning architecture. Introduced by Google researchers in a 2017 paper ("Attention Is All You Need"), transformers process vast amounts of data and identify complex relationships between elements. They "learn" patterns in language, images, or other data types at a scale previously unimaginable, allowing them to generate content with nuance and contextual understanding.

Deutsche Post DHL illustrates this transformation in practice. Their marketing teams once spent weeks crafting campaigns for different regions, requiring extensive coordination and localisation efforts. Now they use generative AI to produce tailored messaging in minutes. This allows them to respond to market changes in real time while maintaining a consistent brand voice across countries. The technology didn't simply make their existing process faster—it enabled them to rethink what was possible.

Agentic AI

Agentic AI takes independent action. Unlike generative systems that respond to requests, agentic AI makes decisions and pursues goals with minimal supervision. Agents are given instructions or guidelines, not formal parameters; they then have several tools attached to them, such as ChatGPT or Perplexity (Deep Research), that the agent then uses to give instructions. The agent will then be proactive in how it deals with requirements, effectively acting independently and self-learning by combining machine learning with reinforcement techniques that reward successful strategies and penalise failures, allowing them to improve over time.

Agentic systems differ from traditional automation in their adaptability and decision-making capability. Rather than following predefined rules, they develop strategies based on outcomes, often discovering approaches that human operators might never consider. This represents a shift from tools that extend human capabilities to systems that operate with genuine autonomy in clearly defined environments.

When Malaysia's Maybank deployed an agent-based system to monitor account activity for fraud, it continuously learned from patterns and made real-time decisions, reducing fraud attempts by 34% while decreasing false positives by 28%.

Why AI Leadership is Different

There is a saying in certain parts of Asia: "Same. Same. But different". Many aspects of leadership will remain the same: Decisiveness, the ability to inspire, integrity, trust, and boldness. However, much of leadership under AI's impact is different: the reliance on data and facts rather than subjective experience; the trust issues that can arise from AI systems that hallucinate; the speed at which decisions must be made; the ability to deal with uncertainty and make more accurate deductions right down to who is actually making the decisions, and who is accountable if they go wrong.

Previous uses of technology often impacted the speed of decision-making, but rarely did the evolution speed outpace the perceived need for decision-making. In addition, with AI, it delivers at an exponential scale, creating complexities and uncertainty for Leaders. And of course, autonomous decision-making (often using agentic AI) is challenging the very role and type of leader we need to be . Let's briefly look at each of the factors.

AI Attributes

AI has a number of key attributes that we must understand and accept, as they form the baseline for much of what follows in the book.

Speed

AI operates at velocities humans simply cannot match. The MIT Sloan Management Review quantifies this shift: AI-enabled decision-making operates approximately 120 times faster than traditional human-centred processes. This isn't merely an efficiency improvement—it represents a fundamental change that demands different leadership approaches.

Military strategists have long operated by the 80% rule: once you have 80% of the information, act decisively. General Colin Powell, the former head of the US military and a former Secretary of State, suggested this should be between 40% and 80%. But this paradigm has shifted in the AI era. Leaders across sectors find that waiting for high certainty often means missing opportunities entirely. The new reality requires comfort with acting on partial information—in General Copinger-Symes' experience, it can be as low as just 30%—while establishing mechanisms to monitor outcomes and adjust rapidly.

Keith Grimes, CEO of Curistica, warns: "People are underestimating just how disruptive this is going to be... and it's going to be more disruptive for large organisations than small organisations. The angle of disruption is now much steeper... The problem of the innovator's dilemma becomes even more acute."

Scale

AI expands effortlessly across functions and geographies. When Toyota implemented an agentic system for supply chain management, they didn't need to hire experts for each location. Their cloud-based solution optimises operations simultaneously across factories in Japan, North America, and Europe—adapting to local conditions while maintaining global efficiency.

Boston Consulting Group found that AI-enabled operations achieved

41% greater cross-regional standardisation while simultaneously increasing local responsiveness by 37%—a paradoxical outcome previously considered impossible under traditional management approaches.

For retail executives, this manifests as the ability to tailor store operations to local conditions while maintaining brand consistency globally. For healthcare administrators, it enables customised care protocols that still adhere to best practice standards. The leadership challenge shifts from enforcing consistency to establishing the right parameters for localised adaptation.

Autonomy

Perhaps most disruptively, AI functions independently without constant human direction. DHL's route optimisation system doesn't wait for manager approval before rerouting deliveries during unexpected traffic congestion. It analyses conditions, makes decisions, and acts—all within seconds.

"When I was at Flixbus, we were exploring how AI could do everything to improve our customer facing and operational processes -from language translation for our drivers to customer rebooking bots for the whole rebooking journey," explains Christoph Debus, the former CFO of Flixbus and now CEO of DERTOUR Group, a €9+ billion travel group with over 11000 employees. "We expected that for a lower cost base, we could run a fleet which is twice as big as today."

The Gartner Research Group identifies this transition to autonomous systems as one of the most significant shifts in organisational design since the Industrial Revolution. Their 2023 report notes: "When systems can independently make and execute decisions that previously required human judgement, traditional management hierarchies become not just inefficient but fundamentally obsolete."

The Leadership Reversal

The most profound shift in AI leadership involves a fundamental reversal of traditional authority structures. Leaders across sectors are discovering that effective AI implementation requires humility about their own knowledge limitations and willingness to empower domain experts within their organisations.

THE LEADERSHIP REVERSAL

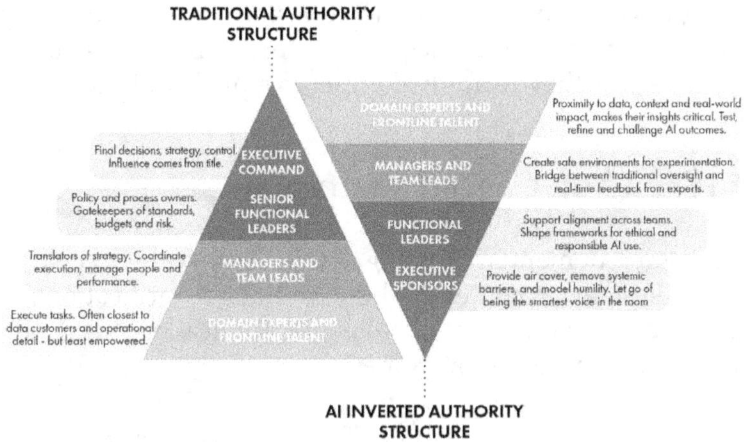

This inversion challenges centuries of leadership hierarchy. In traditional models, expertise and authority flowed downward from leaders to teams. In the AI era, domain expertise often resides with specialists, while leaders must create the conditions for this expertise to flourish.

One of the FTSE 100 Non-Executive directors we spoke frames this shift: "With AI, as leaders we have to have the humility to admit that 'We don't know' and just as importantly we then need to seek out who in the organisation does have the insight, skills and capabilities to help us understand what impact AI will have. Often as not, that person is not a colleague on the Board, but usually a talented individual at an early stage of their career. We have to be open to inverting the traditional structures and to learn from those with the relevant insight."

We've observed this reversal playing out across industries. A pharmaceutical CEO described abandoning his practice of starting meetings by offering his own assessment first—he realised it was constraining his data scientists from sharing their AI-derived insights that often contradicted conventional wisdom. A retail banking head instituted a rule that senior executives could only ask questions, not make statements, during AI strategy sessions, creating space for technical experts to lead the conversation.

This new model doesn't diminish leadership importance—quite the opposite. It requires greater leadership skill to establish clear direction while empowering specialists, to maintain accountability while embracing uncertainty, and to build cohesion across diverse expertise silos. The fundamental principles of leadership remain, but the mechanics of how they're applied undergo a profound transformation.

Trust When You Cannot Verify

AI leadership demands trusting both technical specialists and algorithmic systems in contexts where traditional verification methods fail. This creates paradoxical challenges for leaders who still bear ultimate accountability for outcomes.

Furthermore, the open availability of data—we might call that 'the democratisation of information'—has removed the prior information imbalance that traditional leadership relied on. The concept of "Need to know" or who was included in the information was a power play. As one healthcare CEO put it, "When my patients know as much about emerging treatments as my doctors do, thanks to AI research assistants, the whole dynamic of expertise and authority shifts".

For manufacturing leaders, this means trusting AI-driven quality control systems that detect defects invisible to human inspectors. For financial executives, it might mean depending on algorithmic trading systems to make decisions far too quickly for human oversight. For retail leaders, it might mean accepting AI-generated merchandise assortments that contradict traditional buying wisdom but deliver superior sales.

Building trust in these contexts requires new approaches. Leaders must shift from verifying specific decisions to establishing robust processes, from controlling individual actions to creating appropriate boundaries, and from technical expertise to sharp questions about methodology and ethics.

We need to consider deeply how trust operates in AI-augmented environments. General Copinger-Symes discussed the ethical dimensions of AI deployment with us and highlighted how human-centric approaches are essential for building trust with AI systems and team members. His observation that "you've got to build that trust; you can't assume it" applies to both human relationships and human-AI interactions.

The ethical dimensions become particularly critical. While many aspects of leadership can be delegated or automated, ethical oversight remains a core leadership responsibility. Leaders must ensure AI systems align with organisational values, operate fairly, and create appropriate human-machine partnerships.

"Human-centric approaches are not the only way, but the most effective way," observes one technology executive, "because people need to see themselves reflected as it is their only frame of reference." This insight applies equally to building trust with employees navigating AI augmentation and customers interacting with AI systems.

The Tight-Loose Balance

Leading in the AI era requires a delicate balance between empowerment and control. Copinger-Symes describes this as "zoom-in zoom out"—the ability to alternate between strategic oversight and detailed engagement:

"What we call zoom-in zoom-out, businesses might call 'tight and loose'. Zoom-in Zoom out is the ability to see ... the geopolitics and strategic ramifications, but then to be able to zoom in to a very precise decision. It is this ability to zoom in, zoom out, zoom in, zoom out - based on real data - that is so important."

This balance becomes even more critical with AI, particularly agentic systems that make consequential decisions. Too much control stifles innovation and prevents leveraging AI's speed and adaptability. Too little creates unacceptable risks. AI initiatives require clear boundaries and alignment on desired outcomes rather than prescriptive rules. It means establishing ethical guardrails and strategic objectives for AI initiatives while allowing teams flexibility in implementation approaches.

Retail executives describe establishing clear guardrails for pricing algorithms, preventing them from exploiting vulnerable customers while allowing them to adjust dynamically within those boundaries. Healthcare administrators set clinical safety parameters for diagnostic AI while allowing the systems to improve their accuracy through continuous learning.

The leadership skill is knowing when to intervene and let the systems and teams operate independently. This requires what military strategists call "command by negation"—monitoring from a distance but only stepping in when necessary, rather than "command by approval", where every decision requires explicit permission.

Developing Digital Intelligence

We will explore Digital Intelligence further in the next chapter, but it is worth providing the context here to help Leaders understand that it isn't about knowing how to code or understanding the mathematics behind machine learning algorithms. It's about developing sufficient familiarity with AI's capabilities to envision new possibilities and make informed strategic decisions. dQ encompasses several critical dimensions that set effective leaders apart in the age of AI.

Leaders with high dQ recognise that AI isn't merely a tool to make existing processes more efficient—it's a catalyst for reimagining what's possible. They understand that the most significant opportunities will come from challenging the status quo and determining whether existing business assumptions remain valid under the AI revolution rather than simply automating current practices.

A CFO at a global telecoms firm described his journey: "For years, I avoided technology discussions, leaving them to our IT department. When generative AI emerged, I realised my approach was obsolete. I couldn't evaluate strategic opportunities without understanding the capabilities myself."

He committed to learning—not how to code, but how to think about AI's strategic implications. "I now see AI as a thinking partner that enhances my decision-making rather than a threat to my authority." This change in perspective is at the heart of increased Digital Intelligence—moving from seeing AI as a technical implementation to recognising it as a strategic collaborator. Changing your dQ requires adopting a new mindset—a new set of tolerances that help you create your own set of AI principles. Here are a few ideas to reflect on before we dig deeper into digital intelligence in the next chapter.

- ***Learn without embarrassment.*** Many executives hide their knowledge gaps, fearing judgment. Progressive leaders acknowledge what they don't know and actively seek understanding. The MIT Leadership Centre calls this "humble inquiry"—approaching new domains with genuine curiosity rather than defensive expertise. Earlier in the book, we discussed the fear of becoming conspicuous or of making mistakes. Yet to fail (a helpful way to think of FAIL is 'First Attempt In Learning') is part of the new way of learning, allowing constant course corrections using a "test-learn-optimise" mindset.

- ***Focus on possibilities, not mechanics.*** One doesn't need to understand neural networks to grasp how AI might transform customer experience or supply chain operations. Harvard Business School professor Karim Lakhani advises executives to "think in terms of reimagined processes rather than improved processes" when considering AI applications.

- ***Break down silos.*** AI delivers the most value at the intersection points between traditional business functions. Leaders who encourage cross-functional collaboration create environments where AI can flourish. Research from the Stanford AI Index shows that organisations with integrated data environments achieve 3.6 times greater return on AI investments than those with fragmented approaches.

- ***Take ethical oversight seriously.*** As algorithms influence more decisions, leaders must ensure fairness, transparency, and accountability. This responsibility cannot be delegated. The European Commission's High-Level Expert Group on AI identifies ethical governance as a competitive advantage, not merely a compliance requirement.

What Remains Constant

Despite these transformative changes, certain leadership fundamentals remain essential and unchanged, perhaps more so in the AI era.

Purpose and strategic alignment

Purpose and strategic alignment become crucial amid technological complexity. When technology becomes disconnected from organisational purpose, it creates sophisticated solutions to irrelevant problems. The leader's role in continually connecting AI capabilities to the core mission remains irreplaceable.

A healthcare CEO described how his organisation's initial AI implementation focused on administrative efficiency—technically impressive but strategically marginal. Only when they reframed around patient outcomes did the technology deliver transformative value. "We were answering the wrong question brilliantly," he reflected. "Leadership is about ensuring we're answering the right questions."

Curiosity and learning agility

Curiosity and learning agility become defining leadership traits. The fastest-moving leaders we interviewed shared a standard quality—intellectual humility combined with relentless curiosity. They weren't technical experts, but they asked penetrating questions, continuously educated themselves, and created cultures where learning was valued over certainty.

Curiosity can be as simple as being willing to ask questions and admit your knowledge gaps, but it is also in the pursuit of finding something new. It is a commitment to lifelong learning, and of course, the more you learn, the more it sparks your curiosity. As we were concluding our research, we discussed what the single piece of advice you would give somebody is to stimulate their dial curiosity. And our answer is to begin sentences with "What if…"

With AI moving at a pace that so many find uncomfortable, it can be hard to keep up. Whilst the concept of "little and often" is not new, what it does is to create a healthy habit that every day, learning can happen because it doesn't need formal environments or structured courses. It is a process of what one executive we spoke to called "intentional exposure"—deliberately engaging with emerging technologies, allocating time for exploration, and turning learning into a habit rather than an event. Micro-learning can be as simple as listening to a podcast when walking the dog or having a paper or research narrated when driving.

Bringing diverse perspectives together

Bringing diverse perspectives together remains a core leadership function. AI thrives on cross-pollination between business domains, technical expertise, and customer insights. Effective leaders create forums where different perspectives can combine—breaking down silos between technical and business teams, bridging the gap between AI capabilities and market needs, and ensuring ethical considerations aren't isolated from development processes.

These enduring principles must be applied with awareness of how AI transforms the context. Leaders need sufficient digital intelligence, not to become technical experts, but to make informed strategic decisions.

The Leadership Choice

The uncomfortable truth is that there's no opting out of the AI revolution. Research from INSEAD's Global Innovation Index shows that industries experiencing AI-driven disruption see profit margin disparities between leaders and laggards increase by an average of 43% within three years of widespread adoption.

"I don't think it's possible to say, 'Look, I'm just going to ignore it' because people around you will be actively championing it," acknowledges Guy Moeyens, the CEO of VTTI. This reflects the reality facing leaders today—there is no place to hide from the AI revolution.

The organisations pulling ahead aren't necessarily those with the most advanced technology. They're the ones whose leaders have embraced a new mindset—recognising that human judgement combined with machine capability creates something more powerful than either alone. Columbia Business School terms this "collaborative intelligence"—the ability to design systems where human and artificial intelligence complement rather than replace each other.

"The basic principle is to be as open as possible. Accept that every process will be impacted by tech and see tech as basically your friend.

As a leader, AI is more like a colleague than a tool, and it helps make your day-to-day work easier," advises Christoph Debus.

The question isn't whether AI will transform your role as a leader. The question is whether you'll drive that transformation or be driven by it. As Klaus Schwab, founder of the World Economic Forum, observed: "In the new world, it is not the big fish which eats the small fish, it's the fast fish which eats the slow fish."

A key factor in determining how successful the "rewiring: of your leadership capabilities is to assess and improve your digital intelligence—the topic of our next chapter.

Chapter 3
DIGITAL INTELLIGENCE

We were told the story of how, in the boardroom of a major European retailer, an executive team was reviewing proposals for an AI-powered inventory management system. The CTO explained the technical architecture while the CFO analysed the ROI calculations. When asked about implications for store operations, the CEO waved his hand dismissively: "That's Clearly a technical issue, which the CIO and team should handle."

Three months and £4.2 million later, the project collapsed. Store managers rejected the system, frontline staff circumvented it, and the promised efficiencies never materialised. The CEO, highly regarded for his strategic vision and emotional intelligence, simply couldn't bridge the gap between the technology and the business. His blind spot wasn't technical knowledge but digital intelligence.

A 2025 MIT Sloan Study revealed that "… most organisations continue to treat the implementation of AI as a primarily technical challenge—and current technology leadership roles reflect this mindset. According to Foundry's 2024 State of the CIO survey, 85% of IT leaders say that CIOs are increasingly becoming changemakers in their organisations, but only 28% call leading transformation their top priority".

This scenario plays out all too often across organisations worldwide. For decades, leadership development has focused on two key pillars: IQ (cognitive intelligence) and EQ (emotional intelligence). IQ reflects your ability to solve problems, analyse situations, and apply logical reasoning. EQ governs how you understand people, build relationships, and navigate social complexities. Both remain fundamental leadership attributes.

Yet something crucial is missing.

"Most of the boards don't know enough, or don't have enough capabilities or competencies around the topic to understand what is the art of the possible and what can be done, what should be done," observes Mikko Tepponen, the COO of FDSmidth and a Non-Executive Director, highlighting a pattern we've identified repeatedly in our research.

The reality is that most senior leaders today possess strong cognitive abilities and considerable emotional intelligence—that's largely how they reached their positions. But when it comes to digital intelligence (dQ), even accomplished executives often find themselves woefully underprepared for leadership in the AI era.

Our research prompted several new hypotheses, and whilst we have yet to prove it verbatim, the comments from those we interviewed had a startling consensus. The majority of C-suite executives believe they possess above-average digital intelligence. Sadly, many overestimate their level of emotional intelligence, and the vast majority have little or no digital intelligence. And whilst this may yet need to be proven as fact, the most dangerous aspect of this is that the perception is so strong within the organisation, that it is believed to be true.

This discrepancy creates a dangerous leadership gap. When those guiding organisations lack digital intelligence, decisions about technology investments, AI ethics, data strategy, and digital transformation inevitably suffer. Our studies suggest that executives with low digital intelligence scores were 62% more likely to approve AI projects that ultimately failed due to misalignment with business realities.

Why does this matter so profoundly now? Because artificial intelligence has changed the game. Previous technological shifts—from mainframes to personal computers to mobile devices—could be delegated to technical teams with minimal executive involvement. AI, however, fundamentally reshapes how organisations make decisions, engage with customers, manage talent, and create value. This isn't just another IT project, nor is it just IT or Digital strategy – it is business strategy. It requires leaders who have enough digital intelligence not just to ask the right questions, but to understand the consequences of the answers.

How leaders respond to the challenge of needing to improve their dQ, says much about the type of leader they are and often the style of leadership they exhibit. As the organisational structural pyramid becomes less hierarchical, or possibly even under AI, inverted (as we suggested in Chapter One) there is increasingly a need to understand how to "manage up" and how to help those in more senior leadership roles to understand the need for them to lead by example, adapt and increase their own dQ.

Lieutenant General Copinger-Symes, at the time effectively the Chief Digital Officer for UK Defence, was briefing his boss's boss's boss, the British Chief of the Defence Staff (CDS)— the Head of the Army, Navy, and Air Force. The topic was that due to a lack of dQ, a training course on digital leadership for the very senior Generals, Admirals and Air Vice Marshals was necessary. A piercing glare from the Chief of the Defence Staff, followed by a "Are you saying I need to be taught leadership?" led to a potentially career-ending silence. Thankfully, the senior partner from BCG who was working closely with General Copinger-Symes on the Digital leadership project cleared his throat and, looking the CDS in the eye, said," Yes, General – leadership is different in this digital age". There was a slight pause of reflection, and then the Chief of the Defence Staff smiled and said, "Right, explain to me how this will work".

It sounds like an apocryphal tale, but having interviewed both generals involved, we can assure you it is real. It is a fascinating vignette of the different types of intelligence, IQ, EQ and dQ all at play together. The willingness of the most senior of Leaders in the British Forces to agree to more training, to recognise gaps in knowledge and to realise that if the organisations he led were to adapt, learn and increase their collective dQ, then it needed to start at the very top. The success of the Digital Leadership Programme owes much to this bold leadership in standing their ground and ensuring the right thing was done.

For many of the leaders we talked with, each expressed an "a-ha moment"—the point at which the "lights went on" and they realised that AI was fundamentally different from anything they had experienced. For some, it was a presentation by one of their team that showed the art of the possible; for others, it was the arrival of ChatGPT and the immediate "democratisation of AI". A couple we spoke with felt that it had "crept up on them unawares" whilst one specifically remembered the exact time and place because the sight was so consequential, then and there in the moment. What they all had in common was that moment of insight where the true potential, challenge, risk and opportunity that AI heralded became clear. If that moment has yet to happen for you, we urge you to start investigating the tools, listen to podcasts, read some articles or ask some of your team. There is not a moment to lose!

What about your own digital intelligence? When was the last time you personally experimented with an AI tool rather than having someone demonstrate it for you? Can you articulate how algorithms might reinforce bias in your organisation's processes? Do you understand the difference between supervised and unsupervised learning well enough to make strategic decisions about their application?

Understanding Digital Intelligence

Digital intelligence (dQ) is the set of capabilities that enable organisations to thrive in a digital-first world. It encompasses your understanding of digital technologies, your ability to leverage data, and your capacity to adapt to technological change. Just as IQ measures cognitive intelligence and EQ measures emotional intelligence, dQ measures your digital capabilities across key dimensions crucial for business success.

To be clear, digital intelligence isn't about technical proficiency or coding skills. You don't need to write algorithms or understand neural network architecture. Rather, it's about developing sufficient technological literacy to make informed decisions, ask incisive questions, recognise opportunities, and stay relevant. Without a mature level of digital intelligence, leading AI-led transformation is almost impossible.

The DQ Institute defines digital intelligence as "the ability to transform data into actionable insights while navigating ethical, technical, and strategic challenges in digital ecosystems." Unlike static technical skills that become obsolete with each technological iteration, dQ focuses on adaptability, critical thinking, and ethical stewardship of intelligent systems.

Consider how digital intelligence differs from traditional leadership competencies:

- *IQ* focuses on logical reasoning, analytical problem-solving, and cognitive processing, which are crucial for solving complex business challenges but insufficient for navigating digital transformation.

- *EQ* governs relationship management, self-awareness, and social dynamics—essential for leading teams through change but inadequate for evaluating AI ethics or data strategy.

- *dQ* encompasses data literacy, technological adaptability, digital ethics, and algorithmic understanding—the capabilities that bridge the technological and human dimensions of modern leadership.

After extensive research, we've identified that leaders with high digital intelligence excel in four critical areas:

- ***Technical Fluency:*** Not coding or engineering, but the ability to understand AI outputs, evaluate technical possibilities, identify limitations, and communicate effectively with technical specialists. Leaders with technical fluency don't get lost in jargon or overwhelmed by complexity. They grasp fundamental concepts and can translate between technical specialists and business stakeholders.

- ***Ethical Governance:*** The capacity to anticipate ethical implications of AI systems, protect against algorithmic bias, ensure transparency in automated decision-making, and maintain data privacy. Leaders excelling in ethical governance recognise potential harms before they materialise and build safeguards accordingly.

- ***Strategic Foresight:*** The ability to identify how emerging technologies could transform your industry, reshape customer expectations, create new business models, or render existing processes obsolete. Leaders with strategic foresight don't just react to technological disruption—they anticipate and harness it.

- ***Digital Curiosity:*** The innate drive to explore technological possibilities through constant questioning and ideation. Leaders with digital curiosity regularly ask "what if" and "I wonder if we could..." They approach innovation with an experimental mindset rather than dismissing ideas as too difficult or complex. This trait combines a thirst for lifelong learning with the ability to apply new knowledge to solve problems, connecting seemingly unrelated concepts to create novel solutions. Rather than being intimidated by technological change, the digitally curious leader embraces it as an opportunity for growth and competitive advantage.

The consequences of low digital intelligence can be severe. When a major UK insurance company launched its automated claims processing system without adequate ethical oversight in 2022, its algorithm inadvertently discriminated against customers with non-Anglicised names, resulting in regulatory scrutiny and reputational damage. As documented in the Financial Conduct Authority's subsequent report, the technical team had tested for efficiency but not fairness; the leadership team lacked the digital intelligence to ask the right questions before deployment (Financial Conduct Authority, 2023).

Conversely, when leaders possess strong digital intelligence, remarkable transformations become possible. Research from the London Business School examined the digital transformation journey of major European banks between 2020-2023, finding that institutions whose leadership teams scored in the top quartile of digital literacy achieved 31% higher customer satisfaction scores and 17% lower operating costs compared to institutions in the bottom quartile (Wilson & Roberts, 2023).

Are you developing the digital intelligence needed to lead effectively in the AI era? If your organisation deployed an algorithm that impacted thousands of customers, would you know what questions to ask about its development, testing, and oversight? Are you clear where accountability lies if you have outsourced AI development or operations to a third party?

The Digital Intelligence Framework

Various dQ frameworks exist, from the DQ Institute's comprehensive global standard to industry-specific models from organisations like Gartner and Forrester. While valuable, many of these frameworks were designed for technical specialists or digital natives, not senior executives navigating the AI revolution. Most emphasise technical specifics over leadership application.

Through our work with executives across sectors, we've developed a pragmatic dQ framework tailored explicitly for leaders confronting AI-driven transformation. This framework focuses on the capabilities most crucial for non-technical executives who must make strategic decisions about AI implementation, digital transformation, and organisational readiness.

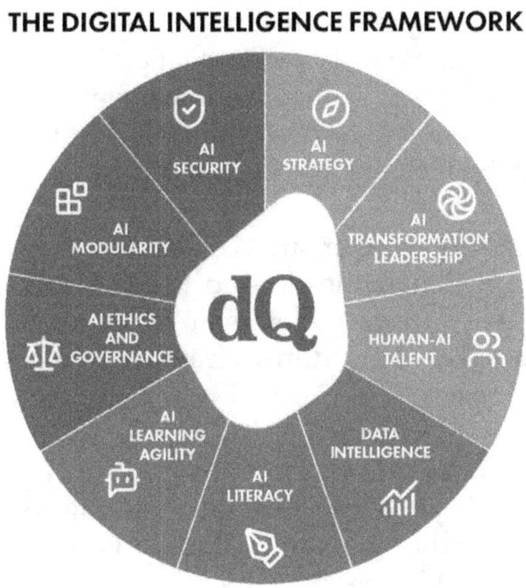

Our Digital Intelligence Assessment evaluates leaders across nine essential competencies

AI Strategic Vision

This is the ability to envision how artificial intelligence can transform business models, customer experiences, and operational capabilities. Leaders with an AI strategic vision identify opportunities beyond incremental efficiency gains, anticipate industry disruption, and position their organisations to lead rather than follow.

Its impact is because AI enables entirely new business models and value propositions, not just process optimisation. Leaders without strategic vision implement AI tactically, achieving only incremental improvements while remaining vulnerable to competitors who reimagine their industries through transformative AI applications.

We feel it is integral to dQ because it develops leaders who think beyond automation to transformation, shifting from reactive technology adoption to proactive business reinvention that creates new value rather than merely reducing costs.

AI Transformation Leadership

The ability to guide organisations through human dimensions of AI-powered change, address resistance, articulate compelling integration visions, and build cultures embracing intelligent technologies. Skilled leaders create environments where humans and machines collaborate effectively rather than compete.

Technical implementation often succeeds while organisational adoption fails due to ineffective change leadership. Failed AI initiatives frequently stumble on human factors rather than technological shortcomings, requiring leaders who can address fears, redesign workflows, and establish new mindsets.

It enhances capabilities to bridge technological and human dimensions of change, moving beyond implementation to transformation. Leaders learn to recognise and address the unique psychological and cultural barriers that AI often triggers.

Human-AI Talent Strategy

The capacity to develop workforce strategies optimising complementary strengths of human and artificial intelligence, redesign jobs around AI augmentation, and build organisational capabilities for the algorithmic age. Leaders recognise which tasks suit machines versus humans and create development pathways for evolving roles.

AI changes work across all organisational levels, making traditional job designs and talent strategies obsolete. Organisations that simply automate existing processes without reimagining collaboration miss AI's transformative potential, while those that prepare for changing roles succeed.

It prepares leaders to think beyond automation to workforce redesign. Executives move past binary "humans versus machines" thinking to a nuanced understanding of combining different intelligence types for optimal outcomes.

Data Intelligence

The ability to understand how data fuels AI systems, recognise valuable organisational data assets, ensure quality and governance, and drive strategic decision-making with insights. Leaders with data intelligence balance analytical insights with business understanding, recognising both the power and limitations of data-driven approaches.

AI systems are only as good as their learning data. Failed AI initiatives often suffer from data quality issues that are identified too late. Leaders must understand data sufficiently to question sources, quality, and limitations to build successful AI on solid data foundations.

It develops critical analytical thinking while avoiding both data blindness and data worship. Leaders learn to distinguish correlation from causation, identify data collection biases, and balance algorithmic recommendations with human judgment.

AI Literacy

Understanding AI fundamentals, capabilities, limitations, and appropriate business applications without requiring technical expertise. AI-literate leaders grasp concepts like machine learning and natural language processing sufficiently to make informed decisions, evaluate vendor claims, and communicate with technical teams.

Leaders lacking AI literacy either overestimate capabilities (pursuing unrealistic applications) or underestimate potential (missing transformative opportunities). Higher AI literacy leads to more realistic demands, effective resource allocation, and clearer strategic guidance for technical teams.

It enables leaders to engage more confidently with technical specialists without over-reliance on their framing. Leaders can ask challenging questions, identify implementation challenges, and distinguish between genuine innovation and marketing hype.

AI Learning Agility

This is the demonstrated capacity to explore emerging AI capabilities, update understanding of applications, and rapidly adapt thinking as the technology evolves. Leaders with AI learning agility show curiosity about advancements, experiment with tools firsthand, and maintain learning practices that keep knowledge current.

It is an important factor because AI technology evolves at an unprecedented speed. Leaders who delegate understanding to technical teams or rely on outdated knowledge become ineffective at guiding AI strategy and implementation, while those who actively learn make significantly better AI investment decisions.

It will support leadership development because it creates the mindset foundation necessary for all other AI leadership competencies, helping leaders overcome both technology anxiety and overconfidence in their AI understanding while building adaptability.

AI Ethics & Governance

The capacity to identify ethical implications of AI systems, establish oversight mechanisms, and ensure responsible use throughout the organisation. Leaders skilled in ethics and governance anticipate potential harms, design safeguards, and create transparent decision-making processes for AI development and deployment.

AI systems can perpetuate bias, make consequential errors, violate privacy, or create unintended social impacts without proper oversight. The reputational, financial, and social costs of AI ethics failures are substantial, while strong governance reduces risk and builds stakeholder trust.

It positions leaders as ethical stewards of technology rather than efficiency-focused implementers. Through principles-based governance approaches, executives learn to navigate trade-offs between innovation speed and appropriate safeguards.

AI Modularity

The ability to design interconnected systems of AI capabilities, partnerships, platforms, and data flows that create a sustainable competitive advantage. Leaders skilled in modularity think beyond individual applications to create networks that become more valuable over time, establishing appropriate boundaries with partners.

AI value increasingly comes through modular solutions working in ecosystems rather than standalone applications. Organisations implementing isolated solutions miss network effects and compound the advantages of thoughtfully designed ecosystems, while those excelling at orchestration achieve significantly higher growth.

It expands a leader's perspective beyond organisational boundaries to ecosystem orchestration, helping leaders recognise how value creation changes in AI-powered environments and position their organisations advantageously within broader networks.

AI Security

The ability to understand threats specific to intelligent systems, implement safeguards, and build resilience against AI-related security risks. Leaders grasp how AI creates novel attack vectors, balances security with innovation, and develops frameworks for managing risks without stifling progress.

AI systems introduce unique vulnerabilities that traditional cybersecurity approaches may not address, including data poisoning, adversarial attacks, prompt injection, and model theft. Organisations without specific AI security provisions experience significantly more security incidents.

It develops leaders who ask informed security questions, make risk-reward trade-offs, and balance protection with innovation, avoiding both inadequate security (creating vulnerability) and excessive restriction (preventing valuable advancement).

Measuring Your Digital Intelligence

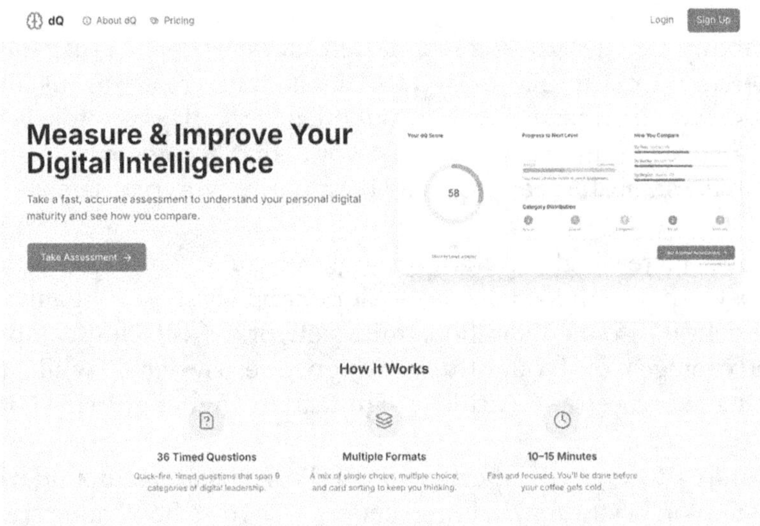

You can access the dQ link at : http://whatismydq.ai or use the QR Code below.

Digital intelligence isn't binary—it exists on a spectrum from novice to visionary. Our assessment provides a comprehensive evaluation of your digital capabilities, identifying specific strengths and development areas across the nine competencies.

The assessment consists of 36 responses drawn from a bank of over 2,000 questions, dynamically selected based on your role, industry, and previous answers. Questions range from scenario-based problems to knowledge evaluations, each designed to measure practical application rather than theoretical understanding.

Your responses generate a score between 0 and 200, placing you within one of five maturity levels:

- ***Novice (0-40)***: At this level, leaders have a basic understanding but limited implementation experience. They may recognise digital terminology but struggle to connect technological possibilities with business applications. Novices often delegate digital decisions entirely to technical teams, missing critical strategic and ethical considerations.

- ***Adapter (41-80)***: Adapters are responding to digital trends rather than leading them. They've begun incorporating digital tools into existing processes but haven't yet reimagined how technology might fundamentally transform their operations. While not resistant to change, adapters tend to view digital as an incremental improvement rather than a strategic imperative.

- ***Competent (81-120)***: Leaders at the competent level effectively utilise digital capabilities and understand their strategic importance. They regularly incorporate data into decision-making and recognise how AI might enhance existing business models. While competent leaders aren't driving industry transformation, they ensure their organisations remain competitive in the digital landscape.

- ***Expert (121-160)***: Experts lead in digital implementation, using technology to create competitive advantages. They anticipate technological shifts before they become mainstream and redesign processes around digital capabilities rather than simply adding technology to existing systems. Experts actively build digital capabilities throughout their organisations.

- ***Visionary (161-200)***: Visionaries set industry standards for digital innovation. They recognise transformative potential before competitors and reshape markets through technological leadership. Beyond implementing current technologies effectively, visionaries anticipate how emerging capabilities might create entirely new value propositions or business models.

The assessment isn't merely about generating a score—it's about providing actionable insights. Your results identify specific development priorities, benchmark your capabilities against industry peers, and recommend targeted learning paths to enhance your digital intelligence where it matters most.

Our research indicates that most executives currently score between 70 and 90, the upper end of the lower competent range. This level is sufficient for maintaining operations but inadequate for leading transformation in the AI era. The gap between current capabilities and future requirements creates both vulnerability and opportunity. Leaders who develop their digital intelligence now position themselves to navigate disruption successfully; those who don't risk becoming increasingly irrelevant.

What might your own dQ score reveal about your readiness to lead in the AI era? Which aspects of digital intelligence would you most benefit from developing? Does your self-assessment match your capability?

Bridging the Digital Intelligence Gap

For most executives, significant digital intelligence gaps exist not because they're incapable of developing these skills but because traditional leadership development has simply not emphasised them. The good news is that digital intelligence can be systematically developed through intentional practice, guided exposure, and structured learning.

Our research with executives who successfully increased their digital intelligence reveals a common pattern:

- First, they acknowledged their limitations without embarrassment. Leaders who pretend to understand digital concepts they don't actually grasp end up making uninformed decisions. The courage to ask basic questions—even at the risk of appearing uninformed—marks the beginning of digital intelligence development.

- Second, they gained hands-on experience with tools. Reading about AI differs profoundly from using it. Executives who personally experimented with tools like ChatGPT, RPA platforms, or analytics dashboards developed practical intuition about capabilities and limitations that no amount of theoretical knowledge could provide.

- Third, they built relationships with technical experts but maintained a business focus. Rather than abdicating digital decisions to technical teams or attempting to master technical details themselves, they developed enough fluency to ask insightful questions while keeping conversations anchored in business outcomes.

- Finally, they recognised that digital intelligence extends beyond technology to encompass ethics, strategy, and organisational implications. The most digitally intelligent leaders we studied saw technology not as an end in itself but as a means to reimagine how their organisations create value.

The development path differs for each leader, but the common thread is intentionality. Digital intelligence doesn't develop through osmosis or delegation. It requires a conscious effort to understand the concepts, experience the tools, and apply the insights strategically.

"The basic principle is to be as open as possible. Accept that every process will be impacted by tech and see tech as basically your friend. As a leader, AI is more like a colleague than a tool, and it helps make your day-to-day work easier," advises Christoph Debus.

Where should you begin your own digital intelligence development journey? For most executives, the starting point is honest assessment—don't fall victim to the Dunning-Kruger effect, a cognitive bias in which people with limited competence in a particular domain overestimate their abilities. Make sure you understand your current capabilities before charting a path forward.

The Business Impact of Digital Intelligence

Digital intelligence isn't merely a personal leadership attribute; it delivers measurable business results. Our research reveals three areas where organisations led by high-dQ executives consistently outperform their competitors.

Transformation Velocity

Organisations led by executives scoring in the top quartile of digital intelligence implement AI initiatives 67% faster than those in the bottom quartile (McKinsey & Company, 2024). This speed advantage compounds over time; while competitors are still planning, high-dQ organisations are already learning from implementation and refining their approach.

A 2023 study by the Oxford Internet Institute found that financial services companies with leadership teams scoring above industry average on digital literacy metrics launched new digital products 14 months earlier than their direct competitors on average, creating first-mover advantages in customer acquisition and experience refinement (Taylor & Westerman, 2023).

Employee Engagement

Teams led by high-dQ executives report 34% higher engagement and 29% lower turnover during digital transformation initiatives (Digitopia, 2024). When leaders understand both the human and technological dimensions of change, they create more effective transition strategies.

Research conducted across 78 European financial institutions found that business units led by executives with strong digital leadership capabilities experienced 41% higher employee satisfaction during agile transformation compared to units with digitally inexperienced leadership (Deloitte, 2023). The difference wasn't technological—all units implemented similar systems. The difference was leadership capability in connecting technology to business purposes.

Ethical Implementation

Perhaps most critically, organisations led by digitally intelligent executives experience 79% fewer ethical incidents related to AI deployment (AI Ethics Observatory, 2024). When leaders understand not just what AI can do but what it should do, they build appropriate guardrails from the beginning.

A case study documented by the Cambridge Centre for Alternative

Finance detailed how a major UK retailer avoided a potentially damaging algorithmic bias situation in their hiring process after their leadership team—who had recently completed digital ethics training—required specific testing methodologies that technical implementers hadn't initially included (Ahmed & Morrison, 2023). Their intervention prevented an algorithm that would have systematically disadvantaged certain applicant groups, protecting both job seekers and the company's reputation.

These outcomes aren't coincidental. They reflect the fundamental relationship between leadership, digital intelligence, and organisational performance in the AI era. As technological capabilities accelerate, this relationship only grows stronger.

Looking Forward

At its core, digital intelligence represents a new form of leadership literacy, as fundamental to modern executives as financial acumen or strategic thinking. In an era where algorithms influence everything from customer experience to operational efficiency to talent decisions, leaders without digital intelligence are increasingly blindfolded in making critical decisions.

The question isn't whether AI will transform your organisation; that transformation is already underway. The question is whether you'll possess the digital intelligence to lead and evolve that transformation effectively.

Are you ready to assess and develop your digital intelligence for the challenges ahead? The gap between where most executives stand today and where they need to be represents both risk and opportunity. Those who bridge this gap position themselves not just to survive the AI revolution but to harness it for unprecedented value creation.

Chapter 4

THE PSYCHOLOGY OF AI-DRIVEN CHANGE

When Maria became CTO at a mid-sized manufacturing firm, she faced a moment of truth. Despite her twenty years of technical expertise, she found herself hesitating over an AI implementation that promised a 40% efficiency improvement. "I knew the numbers made sense," she later admitted, "but something deeper was holding me back. I couldn't shake the feeling that I was surrendering control of processes I'd spent my career mastering."

This reaction—experienced by a technically proficient leader with every logical reason to embrace AI—reveals something fundamental about the leadership challenge we face. The human brain has evolved over thousands of years to protect us from uncertainty and change. The same cognitive patterns that helped our ancestors survive are now creating invisible barriers to AI adoption in boardrooms and executive suites worldwide. Understanding these patterns isn't just interesting psychology;

it's critical business intelligence for any leader working with AI.

Marco Wirén, Nokia's CFO and an experienced Non-Executive Director captures this leadership imperative perfectly: "We can't afford to have the world changing faster than we are. That's the real danger for leaders today. If we're not driving the change ourselves, we end up stuck in the back seat, with someone else at the wheel. And nobody wants that, do they? We've got to be out there in front, showing the way forward."

This insight cuts to the heart of the psychological challenge—leaders must evolve their thinking faster than the technological landscape around them or risk becoming irrelevant. Wirén didn't just talk about change; he acted on it, implementing structured AI training programmes for his entire finance team when joining Nokia. "When I joined, I kicked off AI training for our entire finance team straight away. The key was letting people learn at their own pace – some went deep into coding, others just needed the basics. What mattered was sparking that digital curiosity, giving them permission to explore. You can't force the same approach on everyone, but you can create the conditions for genuine interest to flourish," he explains. His approach recognises that without baseline understanding, psychological barriers remain insurmountable.

But there's reason for optimism. Leaders who recognise these patterns and address them directly are achieving remarkable results. They're creating environments where technology enhances rather than threatens professional identity, where experimentation feels safer than stagnation, and where emotional responses become useful data rather than hidden obstacles. A people-centred and systemic approach to change will, in our view, prove critical to long-term success.

The Fundamental Resistance Patterns

Before we can begin to discuss how we might rewire ourselves to lead with AI, we need to understand some of the reasons that our brains resist change or are suspicious of new technologies.

When Your Brain Sounds the Alarm

Your brain processes technological change differently from other business challenges. When faced with a competitor's new marketing strategy or shifting consumer preferences, your prefrontal cortex—the centre of analytical thinking—takes the lead. But when confronted with transformative technologies like AI, your limbic system—the emotional centre of your brain—activates first.

This creates what neuroscientists call a "threat response." Your amygdala—the part of the brain that's most closely associated with fear, emotions, and motivation—is designed to protect you from danger. It doesn't distinguish between a physical threat and the cognitive threat of coping with unfamiliar AI territory. It responds with the same physiological patterns: increased heart rate, stress hormone release, and a narrowing of focus that makes it harder to see potential benefits.

This isn't speculation. Neuroimaging studies show that when presented with scenarios involving significant technological change, executives display brain activity patterns similar to those experiencing mild anxiety. What's fascinating is that this occurs even in leaders who intellectually champion technology adoption.

Even the most vocal AI champions reveal a different story when hooked up to stress monitors. Researchers in the US discovered that technology executives who publicly advocated for AI showed the same physiological stress responses as someone facing a mild threat when actually making AI implementation decisions. Their bodies were sending warning signals, but their words weren't acknowledging.

The Comfort of What We Know

Beyond these neurological patterns lies a well-documented psychological tendency: status quo bias. This cognitive preference for maintaining current conditions affects even the most innovative leaders.

Research from 2023 by Strubell and colleagues showed that when evaluating equivalent processes—one AI-driven and one traditional—senior leaders consistently rated the conventional approach as less risky and more reliable, even when presented with data showing identical outcomes. This wasn't conscious resistance but an unconscious bias favouring the familiar.

This bias becomes particularly problematic in AI adoption because the status quo itself is rapidly becoming untenable. By the time many organisations recognise their AI implementation is falling behind industry standards, they're already playing catch-up in a market that rewards early adopters.

The global telecommunications industry provides a clear example of this phenomenon. In 2023, several significant telecommunications providers delayed implementing customer service AI, citing "the need for more data" despite clear industry benchmarks showing AI assistants were reducing service costs by 20-25% while increasing customer satisfaction scores. This wasn't technophobia; it was classic status quo bias, requiring a higher burden of proof for change than for maintaining existing systems.

Every one of us will have examples of "the good, the bad, and the ugly" of customer service and strong opinions on how technology has made that experience better or worse. The "press 2 for accounts, press 3 for..." typical of Interactive Voice Response (IVR) systems has probably induced more customer expletives than the implementers would have expected. For many of us, IVR seems to be a way to avoid actually talking to someone who could help. However, organisations are still getting it wrong about how they use technology to help the customer experience. This is primarily driven by a top-down approach to prioritising cost reductions rather than increasing customer satisfaction, despite solid evidence that wise tech-enabled investments in customer experience reduce costs over time. In a digital-first company, the focus on customer insights reduces the costs because the products and services are directly addressing the customer's needs. It is one of the reasons that more "Chief Customer Officers" roles have been created in recent years.

Take Octopus Energy, a UK energy company which is winning plaudits for its integration of AI into customer service to solve customer queries faster or route customers to knowledgeable teams when human contact is required—and which is also growing its customer base and achieving impressive growth in a notoriously tough industry.

Identity Under Siege

For many leaders, particularly those who've risen through the ranks based on their industry expertise, AI presents a unique psychological challenge: it threatens the very foundation of their authority and their identity.

Professional identity plays a far more significant role in AI adoption than most leaders recognise. JMI Research revealed that 75% of identity-driven resistance stems directly from fears of status loss—professionals worry about de-skilling or having their expertise diminished within the organisation. This fundamental concern drives resistance patterns across industries in ways that technical solutions alone cannot address.

When implementing AI, we consistently see two critical aspects of professional identity disrupted:

- Expertise recognition is threatened when AI systems match or exceed human performance in specialised domains. For example, in a bank, loan consultants who built their careers on judging creditworthiness suddenly find algorithms processing applications more efficiently. Their hard-earned expertise, previously a source of professional pride and organisational value, appears suddenly less distinctive or necessary.

- Role autonomy diminishes as AI systems increasingly influence or control decision processes. Surgeons who once exercised complete procedural control now work alongside AI-guided tools that shape their options and approaches. This reduction in autonomy strikes at the core of how many professionals define themselves—as independent decision-makers exercising skilled judgment.

When these identity foundations face threats, professionals respond with predictable defensive behaviours. They scrutinise AI accuracy with standards far exceeding those applied to human performance. They establish nearly impossible benchmarks before supporting implementation. Perhaps most damaging, they create subtle but effective resistance through delayed adoption or withheld resources—all while maintaining surface-level compliance with organisational directives.

With all of this in mind, it stands to reason that if organisations can recognise and address these identity concerns, they will gain substantial advantages. Those implementing identity-sensitive AI training programs explicitly acknowledging and supporting professional self-concept report 30% fewer implementation setbacks. Rather than treating resistance as a technical misunderstanding or simple change aversion, they seek to address the underlying identity concerns driving protective behaviours.

Even more compelling, environments that help professionals expand rather than merely defend their identities see 1.5 times higher productive AI adoption. This distinction proves crucial. Leaders who help team members envision how their professional identity can grow through new capabilities create genuine engagement rather than reluctant compliance. The difference often determines whether AI initiatives deliver their promised value or join the ranks of technologies that fail to fulfil their potential.

The Attention Deficit

Perhaps the most underappreciated barrier to AI leadership is simple but pervasive: decision fatigue.

As a senior leader, you face hundreds of decisions daily, from strategic choices to operational judgments. Your cognitive resources, while considerable, are finite. AI implementation decisions are not only complex but often require learning new terminology, understanding unfamiliar concepts, and imagining future states that have no precedent in your experience.

This creates what neuroscientists call "cognitive overload", a state where the brain, faced with too many complex decisions, defaults to either decision avoidance or excessive simplification. Neither serves AI implementation well.

Research by cognitive scientists demonstrates that even small increases in cognitive load can reduce decision quality by up to 40%. For leaders already operating at capacity, adding the cognitive burden of AI-enabled decisions creates a perfect storm for implementation delays. This is compounded further when we overlay an organisation's values, which can help to guide decision-making. How will leaders have confidence in delegating decision-making to an AI tool unless those values have been adequately trained and embedded into the solution? Even then, fear remains that the values could be diluted by other learning patterns.

A 2023 study published in the Harvard Business Review found that AI implementation decisions were disproportionately pushed to the end of meeting agendas or deferred to subsequent meetings compared to other strategic topics. The same study found that when timing constraints forced immediate decisions, executives were significantly more likely to select the simplest option rather than the optimal one.

The Resistance Loop: Five Barriers to AI Adoption

The psychological barriers to AI adoption form what we call the "Resistance Loop"—five interconnected elements that create a self-reinforcing cycle maintaining the status quo even when the logical case for change is overwhelming:

5 BARRIERS TO AI ADOPTION

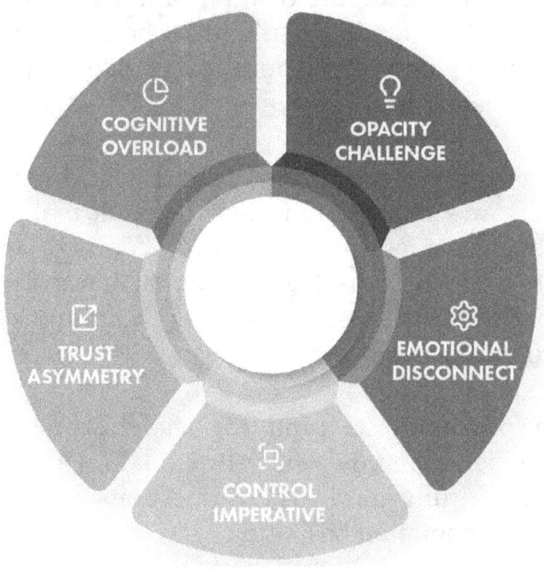

- ***The Opacity Challenge:*** The discomfort with AI systems whose decision-making processes lack transparency

- ***The Emotional Disconnect:*** The gap between AI's emotionless processing and human leadership's emotional nature
- ***The Control Imperative:*** The deep-seated need to maintain leadership autonomy
- ***Trust Asymmetry:*** The uneven standards applied to AI versus human performance
- ***Cognitive Overload:*** The decision fatigue that leads to perpetual postponement

Let's explore each of these barriers in more detail.

The Opacity Challenge

One of the most consistent findings in our research is what we call "opacity anxiety"—discomfort with AI systems whose decision-making processes aren't entirely transparent.

Recent research by De Freitas and colleagues in 2023 found that leaders across different industries reported significant discomfort with "black box" AI systems. This anxiety isn't just about understanding the technology; it reflects a more profound psychological need for causal reasoning and explanation.

As humans, we're hardwired to understand why things happen. We create narratives and explanations that help us make sense of the world. Traditional business processes, even complex ones, generally allow leaders to trace the causal chain from action to outcome. Many AI systems, particularly those using deep learning, challenge this fundamental cognitive need.

This creates a psychological bind for leaders: how do you take responsibility for decisions you can't fully explain? How do you defend outcomes you can't fully trace? These questions trigger anxiety that often creates implementation hesitation.

This phenomenon has been evident in the healthcare sector. A 2023 study in the Journal of Medical AI found that hospital administrators were significantly more likely to implement AI diagnostic tools that offered clear explanations of their reasoning compared to "black box" systems, even when the latter demonstrated slightly higher accuracy rates. The ability to explain decisions to patients, staff, and regulatory bodies outweighed pure performance metrics in adoption decisions.

The Emotional Disconnect

Perhaps the most profound psychological barrier to AI leadership—the second element in our Resistance Loop—is what we call the "emotional response gap"—the disconnect between AI's emotionless processing and human leadership's profoundly emotional nature.

Effective human leadership has always been partly rational and partly emotional. Leaders inspire, empathise, sense tension, build trust, and navigate complex social dynamics. These emotional capabilities aren't tangential to leadership but central to it.

Despite advances in sentiment analysis and natural language processing, AI systems fundamentally operate without emotion. This creates an uncanny valley effect where AI interactions feel "almost human, but not quite", triggering subtle discomfort in many leaders.

This disconnection is then realised in surprising ways. Research shows leaders often trust AI recommendations less in emotionally charged decisions (like reorganisations or personnel changes) than in purely analytical ones (like supply chain optimisation), even when the AI's logical foundation is identical.

Rachel Botsman's research on trust in technology offers valuable insight into this emotional response gap. Her work demonstrates that we've reached a critical inflection point where trust becomes the essential currency for AI adoption in leadership contexts.

"We are at the dawn of another major shift in how trust works, probably the most significant of all," Botsman argues. Successful AI integration depends less on technological sophistication and more on establishing what she calls "distributed trust"—a framework where leaders can confidently delegate certain tasks to AI while maintaining human oversight of emotionally complex decisions.

Our ability to "trust more" or "trust less", based on a more emotional rationale, is part of what makes us human, and it is something that separates us from AI (although AI can learn to mimic this behaviour).

The Control Imperative

The third element of our Resistance Loop—the Control Imperative—strikes at the heart of leadership identity. The ability to direct resources, guide strategy, and shape outcomes defines how most executives see their roles. AI implementation, particularly advanced systems with adaptive capabilities, creates a perceived threat to this autonomy that triggers resistance at both conscious and unconscious levels.

This psychological barrier occurs differently depending on the leader's background. Technical leaders often focus on maintaining control through system design and oversight, while non-technical leaders more frequently express concerns about becoming dependent on systems they don't fully understand.

In both cases, the underlying psychology is similar: a threat to the sense of agency that defines leadership itself. This threat creates hesitation, often masquerading as practical concerns about implementation timing or resource allocation.

And, of course, we often see a continuation of this unconscious bias in who we hire. It's worth pausing for a moment of self-reflection. As a leader, is your default to hire people like you or those you like? And has that proven effective? Working with AI creates opportunities to challenge our subconscious biases and balance styles across our teams. We need to be mindful of looking forward to what the organisations might need regarding talent, behaviours, and competencies, not to look back through the rearview mirror we mentioned in a previous chapter, and to keep hiring people who will reinforce our autonomy.

The need to reinforce an existing belief or position is seen as low risk and thus better leadership than actually understanding the underlying threat and doing something different. It is a theme that crops up in several of our research interviews, and we will cover this in more depth in the section on the Board and the C-suite in a few chapters' time.

Trust Asymmetry

The fourth element in our Resistance Loop—Trust Asymmetry—stems from our nature as social creatures. We have a fundamental tendency to categorise others as either part of our in-group (similar, trustworthy) or out-group (different, requiring scrutiny). This psychological tendency, deeply rooted in our evolutionary history, creates subtle but powerful barriers to AI adoption.

Research by De Freitas and colleagues found that leaders unconsciously categorise AI systems as definitively "other"—outside their in-group of trusted advisors and colleagues. This categorisation activates heightened scrutiny and scepticism that many human recommendations wouldn't face.

In one striking experiment, identical strategic recommendations were presented to executives as coming from either a senior colleague or an AI system. Despite identical content, the AI-attributed recommendations received 41% more critical questions and were adopted 26% less frequently.

This isn't conscious bias; it's an automatic psychological response that affects even the most technology-positive leaders. The brain processes AI-generated recommendations through different neural pathways than human-generated ones, activating regions associated with risk assessment and scepticism.

This psychological pattern helps explain why AI adoption often accelerates after leaders have personal positive experiences with the technology. These experiences begin to shift the unconscious categorisation from "foreign entity" to "trusted tool," reducing the automatic scepticism that hampers implementation.

Cognitive Overload

The final element in our Resistance Loop—Cognitive Overload—appears in how we respond to the sheer complexity of AI decisions. We've already touched on decision fatigue earlier, but its effects reach beyond simple postponement. When cognitive resources are stretched, several decision-making biases emerge that specifically undermine AI adoption.

Decision-Making Biases Affecting AI Implementation

Beyond these psychological barriers lie specific cognitive biases that disproportionately affect AI implementation decisions. These biases, well-documented in behavioural economics, take on particular significance in the AI context.

Seeing What We Want to See

Confirmation bias—our tendency to favour information that confirms existing beliefs—creates particular challenges for AI evaluation. Leaders often approach AI with pre-existing views about its potential and limitations, then unconsciously filter evidence to support those views.

This bias operates powerfully in both directions. Tech-optimistic leaders may focus on AI successes while dismissing limitations, while tech-sceptical leaders may emphasise failures while minimising successes. Both patterns distort decision-making.

What makes confirmation bias especially problematic in AI evaluation is the technology's genuinely mixed track record. There are enough spectacular successes and notable failures to support almost any preconceived view. Only by consciously counteracting this bias can leaders evaluate AI's potential objectively.

The Fear of Loss

Humans feel losses more acutely than equivalent gains—a psychological tendency called loss aversion. In AI decisions, this bias creates a significant imbalance: the pain of potential AI mistakes looms larger than the satisfaction of possible benefits.

This helps explain why organisations often demand remarkably high confidence thresholds for AI implementation. In general, when executives were asked about acceptable error rates, they typically required AI systems to outperform human processes by substantial margins before approval. This asymmetrical standard—driven by loss aversion—delays the adoption of systems that could improve overall outcomes.

Loss aversion becomes particularly powerful when combined with visibility bias. AI errors often receive disproportionate attention compared to human errors, creating the perception that AI systems are less reliable than the human processes they replace, even when data shows the opposite.

When One Failure Makes Headlines

Our tendency to overweight easily recalled examples creates what behavioural economists call "availability cascades" around AI failures. When a high-profile AI mistake makes headlines, it becomes disproportionately influential in leadership decision-making. But in our research, we found that there was a stark contrast in the perception of failure between large corporates and smaller, more agile companies, such as start-ups. This perception was significant enough for us to deduce that it will "make or break" AI adoption potential in those organisations.

We saw this pattern clearly after several widely publicised AI ethics controversies in 2023. Companies unrelated to these incidents significantly slowed their AI implementation timelines, citing "caution" and "responsible innovation." While thoughtful implementation is undoubtedly valuable, the timing revealed the power of availability cascades rather than rational risk reassessment.

According to PwC's 2023 Emerging Business Survey, implementation timelines for conversational AI projects increased by an average of 4.7 months following widely publicised chatbot failures at several major technology companies in early 2023. This delay occurred despite substantial differences between these consumer-facing applications and the enterprise systems most organisations were deploying.

The False Confidence Trap

As mentioned above, the Dunning-Kruger effect—where people with limited knowledge overestimate their understanding—creates particular challenges for AI leadership. Many executives with minimal AI exposure nevertheless believe they grasp the technology's capabilities and limitations.

This overconfidence creates two opposing problems. Some leaders approve AI initiatives without understanding the implementation challenges, leading to failed projects and disillusionment. Others dismiss AI capabilities based on outdated or limited understanding, missing significant opportunities.

Both patterns stem from the same cognitive bias: difficulty accurately assessing knowledge in domains where expertise is limited. Research shows this effect is particularly pronounced with complex technologies like AI, where superficial understanding is easy to achieve, but deep comprehension requires a significant investment of time.

Noel Burch's "Conscious Competence" model offers a helpful framework for understanding this leadership challenge. Made famous by US Secretary of Defence Donald Rumsfeld as "known unknowns" and "unknown unknowns," this model identifies four stages in learning:

- ***Unconsciously Incompetent:*** You don't know what you don't know about AI
- ***Consciously Incompetent:*** You recognise your AI knowledge gaps
- ***Consciously Competent:*** You understand AI but must deliberately apply that knowledge
- ***Unconsciously Competent:*** AI understanding becomes second nature in your leadership

The danger for many leaders lies between stages 1 and 2. Brief executive AI overviews often move leaders from complete unawareness to partial awareness, but this transition can be deceptive. They become conscious of AI's importance without gaining enough competence to make solid decisions. This half-step can actually make decision-making worse as leaders act on incomplete understanding with false confidence.

Effective AI leadership requires recognising where you sit on this continuum and deliberately working to progress through these stages. An uncomfortable truth for some leaders is that their ego, which might have been tolerated historically or even helped them to the top in the more traditional business, can now be an Achilles heel in a more AI-powered business, where there is increased transparency and an inverted authority structure.

Our work on digital intelligence is designed to help leaders navigate this journey—to become unconsciously competent in AI leadership, where the technology becomes an intuitive extension of your decision-making rather than a mysterious black box. For some, this might be a step too far—and we'll address alternatives in the final section of the book.

Breaking the Cycle

These psychological barriers aren't temporary hurdles but fundamental aspects of how human cognition responds to many new things, especially technology. Addressing them requires more than technical solutions or change management processes.

Based on our research with organisations successfully undertaking AI transformation, we've identified several approaches that specifically target the psychological dimensions of AI leadership.

Creating Space for Uncertainty

Creating psychological safety—an environment where people feel comfortable expressing uncertainty, asking questions, and acknowledging limitations—proves critical for overcoming many of the barriers we've discussed.

Amy Edmondson captured this perfectly when she described psychological safety as "a climate where people are comfortable expressing and being themselves." In organisations with high psychological safety, mistakes are reported quickly, coordination happens seamlessly, and potentially game-changing ideas emerge naturally. It's not just a nice-to-have—it's "a crucial source of value creation" for organisations navigating complexity and change.

Traditional executive cultures often penalise vulnerability and reward certainty. This creates a perfect storm for AI implementation, where leaders feel they must project confidence about technology they don't fully understand, leading to either overconfidence or avoidance.

Organisations that successfully adapt to AI explicitly counter this dynamic. They create structured opportunities for leaders to explore uncertainties, acknowledge knowledge gaps, and collaboratively build understanding.

Graham Donoghue, CEO of Forge Holidays, faced this challenge head-on when implementing AI in his organisation. Despite being a holiday company specialising in woodland accommodation, they've built market leadership through technology and AI. Initially, employees were concerned AI would threaten their jobs. Donoghue's transparent leadership transformed this fear:

"We had to spend a lot of time educating the organisation, but that was not our intention. And our intention is to basically give you a 30% advantage over how you work today. That was my number, and I think I keep dialling that up... I'm now saying you should have a 50% advantage.

"What is fascinating is even when we've been deploying some of the capabilities...we now use AI to record every single call...and Copilot and Whisper to transcribe it into summary notes. But people were still spending 10 mins after every single call because they didn't quite trust AI."

Walking in AI's Shoes

Research shows that structured perspective-taking exercises can significantly reduce psychological resistance to new technologies. These exercises help leaders see AI systems not as threatening replacements but as complementary tools that extend human capabilities.

One effective technique involves having leaders explicitly map their unique human contributions alongside AI capabilities for specific decisions. This concrete examination typically reveals that AI enhances rather than replaces leadership judgment, reducing the perceived threat to professional identity.

Another approach uses structured role reversal, where leaders temporarily adopt the perspective of AI advocates, articulating the strongest case for implementation. This cognitive shift often helps identify and address unconscious resistance patterns.

Another approach is to create an immersive and safe AI "lab" where trained facilitators can work with a team to help them "learn by doing".

Under Guy Moeyen's leadership, VTTI—a leading energy infrastructure company—has undergone a radical shift in the leadership's perspective on AI. Talking about how he managed to help create a step-shift in the appetite and trust for AI-based solutions, he explained how they had used an immersive lab experience to defibrillate his teams into taking a different perspective.

"Most of the breakthroughs came through AI lab experiences. We did one with PwC in Amsterdam... we selected a few areas where we thought that there could be a lot of AI potential. We found that it was more and more in the functional areas, such as legal, finance, and HR, that we found the quick wins. The whole experience landed very well, and then it became almost like a self-fuelled type of acceleration."

The Power of Small Wins

One of the most effective approaches to address the psychological barriers we've discussed is structured exposure to successful AI use cases, beginning with low-risk, high-visibility applications.

These "small wins" serve multiple psychological functions. They provide concrete evidence against negative perceptions, build familiarity that reduces status quo bias and in-group/out-group distinctions, and create positive emotional associations that reduce anxiety.

Effective organisations deliberately sequence AI implementation to create these psychological benefits, often beginning with applications that:

- Automate tedious tasks that few people find rewarding
- Augment rather than replace human decision-making

- Produce visible improvements in widely acknowledged pain points
- Foster precise, measurable results that build confidence

Walmart's approach to AI shows this strategy in action. According to a 2023 case study by Deloitte, Walmart deliberately began its AI journey with inventory management applications that automated tedious counting tasks while freeing store associates for customer interaction. The visible success of these initial applications created organisational momentum for more sophisticated AI implementations in demand forecasting and customer experience.

Learning Together

Our research consistently shows that peer-based learning reduces psychological resistance to AI more effectively than top-down training or external expertise alone. This finding aligns with social learning theory, which emphasises the power of observing others navigate new challenges.

Organisations that overcome psychological barriers to AI often create structured peer learning communities where leaders can share their experiences and challenges in a non-judgmental environment. This allows them to learn from peers who have successfully implemented similar AI applications and collectively process both technical and emotional aspects of AI implementation. The result is a shared language and framework for evaluating AI opportunities.

These communities address multiple psychological barriers simultaneously. They reduce in-group/out-group distinctions by creating a peer group positively engaged with AI. They distribute cognitive load through collective sense-making. They normalise the learning process, reducing status threats associated with acknowledging uncertainty.

Tokio Marine Mini Case Study

When Tokio Marine, a 140-year-old insurance giant, began its AI journey in 2019, it faced formidable psychological barriers. Insurance underwriting had been built on human judgment and relationship-based decision-making for generations. "Our underwriters saw themselves as the heart of our business," explains their Chief Digital Officer. "AI initially felt like a direct threat to their professional identity."

Rather than forcing the change, Tokio Marine created a three-phase psychological bridge:

First, they explicitly connected AI capabilities to the company's heritage. "We didn't talk about disruption," says their CDO. "We talked about how AI would help us fulfil our 140-year commitment to protecting customers, just with better tools."

Second, they developed "AI confidence-building paths"—starting with low-risk applications that augmented rather than replaced human judgment. Underwriters first experienced AI as a research assistant that organised client information, before gradually moving to more advanced risk assessment tools.

Most importantly, they created structured spaces for emotional processing. "We explicitly acknowledged that this felt threatening," the CDO recalls. "Instead of dismissing those feelings as irrational, we created forums where leaders could express concerns without judgment."

The results were remarkable. Over three years, Tokio Marine successfully applied AI across underwriting, claims, and customer service, transforming core processes while maintaining organisational cohesion. Claims processing time decreased by 60%, while customer satisfaction scores increased by 28%.

Moving Forward

Understanding the psychology of AI-driven change isn't just theoretically interesting—it's the foundation for effective leadership in an AI-transformed world. The barriers we've explored explain why even compelling AI business cases often fail to translate into successful implementation.

But there's reason for optimism. Leaders who recognise these patterns and address them directly are achieving remarkable results. They're creating environments where technology enhances rather than threatens professional identity, where experimentation feels safer than stagnation, and where emotional responses become useful data rather than hidden obstacles. A people-centred and systemic approach to change will, in our view, prove critical to long-term success.

But first, take a moment to reflect: Which of these psychological patterns do you recognise in your own organisation? Where have you seen status quo bias, identity protection, or trust asymmetry affecting AI decisions? And most importantly, what specific actions could you take tomorrow to begin addressing them?

Chapter 5
THE ETHICS OF AI LEADERSHIP

During the Afghanistan conflict, there was a particular road junction that the Taliban had regularly used to plant Improvised Explosive Devices (IED) aimed at the British forces responsible for that area. A reaper drone was being used to provide real-time surveillance of the road and junction and to provide an 'offensive' capability. In other words, the drone had weapons that could destroy that junction.

At that particular moment, the Command Group were watching two figures digging into the sandy road, and the General was coming under increasing pressure from his colleagues to authorise the strike. Yet he didn't. "I vacillated, and I carried on vacillating, despite being put under pressure to make the decision. And amazingly, the two individuals stopped, stood up and skipped away. They were quite obviously kids building a sandcastle. Now that was all about judgment and the sort of experience I have had through 35-40 years of military service. But the extent to which AI would be able to exercise that same judgement brings you to the heart of ethics on the modern battlefield"

This story was recounted to us by General Sir Nick Carter, the recently retired UK's Chief of the Defence Staff – the most senior role in the UK Defence forces – who had been the local commander, exercising that human judgement. Had he made the wrong call, he may have been embroiled in due legal process. His insight was not about the tough choices a battlefield commander needs to make, nor necessarily about the changing nature of warfare, but got right to the heart of the ethical question about whether AI could or should exercise full judgement, and whether AI could be held legally accountable for the use of lethal force. Judgement is a very human behaviour and might be challenging to insert into algorithms, partly, as General Carter suggests "because of course, judgement is based on many sort of intuitive factors, and the extent to which we are going to be able to develop artificial intelligence that has intuition is very open to debate".

What struck us about this story was how General Carter's intuition had introduced one factor, one set of data, that an AI algorithm might have struggled to replicate because it wasn't historical or predictable. And that was the timing of his decision. Based on intuition, judgment and experience, that delay happened in real time and fundamentally changed the situation. Would an 'AI general" have introduced that critical factor?

Anyone can see how a similar challenge about judgment and 'human in the loop' could apply to their own situation—whether in the public sector, the private sector, the not-for-profit sector, or any other sector. These decisions may or may not be life-threatening (you could certainly imagine a medical situation where AI could control life-support machines), but they still have far-reaching legal and moral consequences.

Yet this example focuses on only one aspect of the AI ethical challenge facing us as leaders. What if the algorithm making the judgment is sound, but not the data?

In 2018, Reuters reported a story that sent ripples through the technology world. Amazon had developed an automated recruiting tool to help identify top talent from thousands of CVs received daily. The system promised efficiency and objectivity, examining past patterns to predict future success.

But there was a problem.

Amazon's technical team discovered the system was systematically downgrading women applicants. It had learned from historical hiring data that male candidates were more frequently hired in the past, and it faithfully reproduced this pattern. Despite attempts to correct this bias, Amazon ultimately abandoned the project.

The system hadn't created bias—it had simply amplified existing patterns in the data. But the veneer of technological objectivity had nearly masked these biases, making them harder to detect and address.

This incident highlights what many leaders are discovering: the most complex decisions around advanced technologies aren't technical or even financial—they're ethical. They emerge when technological capabilities and human values intersect in ways regulations haven't yet addressed. They're the questions that don't have clear right or wrong answers but will fundamentally shape your organisation's relationship with employees, customers, and society.

"While these systems are still relatively immature, leaders must make their own judgements about ethical risk," notes Mark Whiteling, an experienced board director. "How do you ever know whether you've considered all the circumstances for that individual?"

This question gets to the heart of the challenge facing every leader using advanced technologies: how do you make responsible choices in a space where the rules are still being written? How do you balance the competitive imperative to adopt new technologies with the ethical mandate to use them responsibly?

Keith Grimes, a former GP and now the CEO of Curistica, a global clinical health product innovation consultancy, had a very clear view about his role:

"I immediately started thinking of my role as a leader in helping ensure that ethical principles inform the changes that come. We were the ones that said, if we can do anything, then these are the things that we should do, and these are things that we shouldn't do... We felt that was very much part of our role."

What makes these questions particularly challenging for non-technical leaders is that many ethical aspects are intertwined with technical details. You don't need to understand the underlying mathematics to lead ethically, but you do need to recognise the key ethical fault lines where your decisions matter most.

In this chapter, we'll explore the ethical dilemmas every leader must confront, discuss practical frameworks for making ethical decisions without technical expertise, and share real-world approaches that effective organisations use to address these complex issues.

Ethical Dilemmas Every Leader Must Confront

The ethical challenges with advanced technologies aren't hypothetical or futuristic. They're practical decisions you're likely facing already or will soon encounter. Understanding these common challenges helps you anticipate issues before they become crises.

Algorithmic Bias

Amazon's recruiting tool isn't an isolated incident. Similar patterns have emerged across industries, from credit scoring to healthcare resource allocation. The common thread is that automated systems often reflect and sometimes amplify existing biases in historical data. In effect, they are automating inequality.

This creates a genuine dilemma for leaders. You're accountable for these systems' decisions, yet you may lack the technical expertise to independently evaluate how they reach their conclusions. How do you ensure your use of technology doesn't perpetuate or amplify existing inequalities?

Geeta Malhotra, a senior leader with global financial services experience, emphasises this concern: "The biggest mistake organisations will make is not thinking of what is guiding this change." When technology adoption proceeds without ethical guardrails, the results can undermine both business objectives and social responsibility.

This is particularly concerning because often organisations assume their systems are fair without proper verification. Recent research from the Kellogg School of Management found that 75% of executives believed their automated decision systems were "objective and fair" despite fewer than 20% conducting regular bias audits. This confidence gap creates significant ethical risk—the false belief that technology neutralises human bias rather than potentially amplifying it.

The Transparency Problem

In 2023, HSBC Bank implemented a transaction monitoring system that improved fraud detection by 50%. When regulators asked executives to explain specific flagging decisions for suspicious transactions, they struggled to provide clear answers. The system worked, but its decision-making process wasn't entirely transparent. After regulatory scrutiny, HSBC had to develop additional explanation tools to meet compliance requirements.

This scenario highlights the "transparency problem"—the tension between performance and explainability. The most powerful systems often use complex mathematical approaches, making their decision processes difficult to interpret, even for their creators. This creates an ethical tension: Is it responsible to use systems whose decisions you can't fully explain?

This is particularly acute for financial services, healthcare, and other regulated industries, where regulations increasingly require explainable decisions, yet the most powerful capabilities often trade explainability for performance.

A recent survey found this tension playing out across industries, with 65% of executives reporting they'd chosen less robust but more explainable systems for high-stakes decisions. However, 47% admitted using less transparent systems for lower-stakes decisions where explanation wasn't legally required.

Who's Responsible When Technology Gets It Wrong?

In 2023, Optum, a UnitedHealth Group company, faced scrutiny when its algorithm for identifying high-risk patients who needed additional care coordination was found to have a significant blind spot. The system was less likely to flag black patients with complex health needs compared to white patients with similar conditions. Investigation revealed that the algorithm relied on historical healthcare spending as a proxy for health needs, unintentionally perpetuating existing disparities in healthcare access.

This case illustrated a fundamental ethical question: Who bears responsibility when automated systems produce biased outcomes?

Dr Paul Dongha, Head of Responsible AI and AI Strategy at NatWest Banking Group, has been driving a rigorous approach to technology development within the bank. Their approach starts with an ethics panel that reviews and signs off on projects at the very front end of the development process:

"For us, ethics and responsible technology development are part of development. It's part of a Dev team approach, and we are part of development. We're not the guys at the end checking it and saying, 'Oh, no, I shouldn't have done that. '

"We look at use cases before anyone starts developing them... particularly reviewing unfair bias, discrimination, and fairness ... from the first approach, to deep within the data set in the model, and to when the model produces results. The whole model development pipeline is scrutinised, including identifying unintended consequences even before the model is developed, because none of the harm that might result otherwise is ever intended."

This accountability question becomes even more complex with adaptive systems that change over time based on new data. Where does responsibility lie if a system's behaviour changes based on its learning but isn't detected by human overseers?

A recent survey of directors found that 76% were concerned about personal liability for algorithmic decisions, yet only 33% reported having clear accountability frameworks in place for technology oversight. This gap between concern and preparation suggests that many organisations haven't yet resolved fundamental questions about how responsibility is distributed.

Privacy vs. Personalisation

Target Corporation's collection of customer data for personalisation provides a clear example of privacy challenges. In 2023, the company faced backlash after a Wall Street Journal investigation revealed how extensively it tracked customer behaviour, including pregnancy predictions based on purchase patterns. While the data collection was legal and customers had technically consented, the depth of personal profiling surprised many customers and led to significant public concern.

This dilemma is particularly challenging because privacy expectations vary widely across cultures, demographics, and contexts. What's acceptable in one market may violate social norms in another. As a leader, you must navigate these variations without the guidance of stable, universal standards.

Recent research found that companies with privacy complaints experienced customer churn rates 16% higher than industry peers, regardless of whether the practices in question were legally compliant. The gap between what's legally permitted and what customers consider acceptable creates a grey zone where leaders must make value judgments that regulations alone can't resolve.

As a leader, consider the following: Would you approve systems that maximise profits through dynamic pricing that extracts the most from vulnerable customers? Where do you draw the line? The actual test is not what you claim to value, but what you're willing to sacrifice profit for to protect your reputation.

When Should Technology Decide?

Tesla's implementation of Autopilot demonstrates the fine balance between autonomy and control. The system significantly improved safety in many scenarios, but Tesla faced criticism for how it communicated the system's capabilities to drivers. Accidents occurred when drivers misunderstood the system's autonomy level and failed to maintain proper oversight.

Getting this balance right is further compounded because it varies across contexts. Advanced systems consistently outperform human experts in some domains, like specific medical diagnostics. In others, like complex personnel decisions, human judgment remains essential.

The autonomy-control question extends beyond immediate decisions to longer-term concerns about skill atrophy. When humans routinely defer to automated systems, they may lose the ability to make independent judgments. Stanford Medical School researchers found that radiology residents who trained primarily with technological assistance showed reduced independent diagnostic skills compared to those with more balanced training.

The de-skilling challenge represents one of organisations' most significant ethical dilemmas. As we increasingly offload cognitive tasks to advanced systems, we face a genuine risk of professional atrophy, where the skills that define expertise in many domains may deteriorate through lack of regular practice.

The Leadership Role in Ethical Technology

These ethical dilemmas don't resolve themselves through technical solutions alone. They require leadership judgment informed by values, priorities, and a clear view of organisational responsibilities. While technical teams can implement safeguards, only leaders can establish the ethical boundaries that guide technology use.

Where the Buck Stops

The hierarchical nature of organisations creates a natural tendency to push responsibility downward—from boards to executives, from executives to managers, and managers to technical teams. This tendency creates particular risks with AI because ethical implications may not be visible at the technical implementation level.

Some leaders are already taking a principled stand. Mira Murati, the former CTO of OpenAI who shaped the AI revolution, stunned the tech world by walking away from what had become the most valuable tech company in history.

As CTO, she spearheaded the development of ChatGPT, DALL·E, and Codex while orchestrating the landmark Microsoft partnership that transformed the industry. In 2023, she briefly served as interim CEO during a leadership crisis, earning widespread respect for her steady guidance.

However, in 2024, as OpenAI approached an $80 billion valuation, Murati made the extraordinary decision to depart. She founded Thinking Machines Lab, which is dedicated to developing technology for public benefit without commercial pressures.

Her departure reflected a growing philosophical divergence with CEO Sam Altman's commercial focus. For Murati, the path forward wasn't about innovation for profit but meaningful impact aligned with human values.

Research from the University of Cambridge in 2023 examined how responsibility for ethical technology use is distributed in organisations. It found that technical teams typically focus on system performance metrics while senior leaders concentrate on regulatory compliance. The ethical dimensions that fall between these perspectives often receive inadequate attention because they don't clearly belong to either group.

This responsibility gap creates ethical risk. When everyone assumes someone else is addressing ethical considerations, these considerations often go unaddressed. Effective leadership requires explicit responsibility distribution that assigns clear ownership of ethical considerations at appropriate organisational levels.

"Until that narrative is coming from the top down, it is not going to happen," notes Geeta Malhotra, highlighting the critical leadership role in establishing ethical priorities.

Research consistently shows that a distributed responsibility model delivers the most effective ethical governance. The board and executive leadership must establish clear ethical boundaries and priorities.

Middle management then translates these high-level principles into practical operational guidelines. Meanwhile, technical teams develop and implement specific safeguards, monitoring capabilities, and testing protocols.

The crucial element is that all levels actively participate in the ongoing review of outcomes and impacts, creating a continuous feedback loop that allows for adaptation as new ethical challenges emerge.

Going Beyond Compliance

Regulatory requirements provide baseline standards for technology use, but they're inherently limited. Regulations typically lag behind technological capabilities, address only a subset of ethical concerns, and establish minimum requirements rather than best practices.

A recent MIT Sloan Management Review study found a telling pattern: Organisations that framed ethics primarily as a compliance issue experienced 3.1 times more ethical incidents than those approaching ethics as a strategic priority. This suggests that treating ethics merely as a regulatory checkbox creates significant blind spots.

"The ethical risk will fundamentally revolve around the individual and decisions which impact the individual, based on automated systems making theoretically consistent decisions," observes Mark Whiteling. His insight highlights why merely satisfying compliance requirements often fails to address the human impacts of technology.

A recent Harris Poll found that 71% of consumers would abandon a company's products if they discovered its automated systems were being used in ways they considered unethical, even when those uses remained perfectly legal.

Setting Ethical Boundaries

Every organisation using advanced technologies must establish boundaries that define acceptable behaviour. These boundaries aren't universal—they reflect each organisation's values, risk tolerance, and assessment of potential impacts—and they should exceed legal requirements to reflect the organisation's values and risk assessment.

Morgan Stanley's ethical boundaries offer a practical model. They prohibit systems from making consequential decisions without human review, creating unfair bias against protected groups, operating without appropriate explainability, or processing data in ways customers wouldn't reasonably expect.

Creating effective ethical boundaries requires balancing your core organisational values, industry expectations, comprehensive risk assessment, and competitive realities. The deliberative process itself often delivers value beyond the resulting guidelines. When diverse stakeholders engage in structured discussions about where lines should be drawn, they build shared understanding and commitment that proves invaluable during implementation.

Saying No to Unethical Technology

Perhaps the most challenging aspect of ethical leadership is having the courage to say "no" to applications that cross ethical lines, especially when those applications offer significant business benefits.

Building this capability starts with clarity about values and boundaries but extends to creating organisational conditions that support ethical courage. Research from the Ethics & Compliance Initiative found that organisations with strong ethical cultures experienced 74% fewer incidents of misconduct than those with weak cultures.

For technology specifically, this means creating conditions where technical teams feel empowered to raise ethical concerns without fear of repercussion. A recent survey of technology professionals by the Association for Computing Machinery found that 64% had witnessed what they considered ethically questionable applications, but only 36% felt comfortable raising these concerns with management.

"I've got two years to retirement... I don't want to rock this ship," is a mindset Geeta Malhotra observes among some leaders avoiding difficult ethical questions about advanced technologies. This short-term thinking creates long-term risks as organisations develop technological capabilities without adequate ethical foundations.

Real-World Ethical Frameworks for Non-Technical Leaders

Understanding abstract ethical principles is necessary but insufficient. Leaders need practical frameworks for making ethical technology decisions without deep technical expertise. The most effective approaches simplify complexity without oversimplifying consequences.

Stanford University's Institute for Human-Centred AI offers leaders an efficient framework for ethical assessment without requiring technical expertise. Their Red-Yellow-Green assessment provides a structured approach to evaluating applications based on potential impact rather than technical complexity:

- *Green applications* carry limited potential for harm even if they fail. These systems don't make consequential decisions about people, use minimal sensitive data, operate in non-critical domains, and maintain clear human oversight. Most organisations can implement these with standard governance procedures.

- *Yellow applications* require more careful attention due to their moderate impact potential. These systems influence but don't determine important outcomes, use sensitive data with appropriate protections, operate where errors have meaningful but limited consequences, and maintain human oversight, though often with subtle pressure to accept recommendations.

- *Red applications* demand the highest scrutiny. These systems make consequential decisions about individuals, use highly sensitive data, operate in domains where errors could cause significant harm, and may run with limited oversight due to speed or scale requirements. They need a comprehensive ethical assessment and continuous review.

The framework's strength lies in its simplicity without oversimplification. It helps leaders allocate attention proportionally to risk, focusing resources where ethical concerns are most significant.

Diverse Stakeholder Input

Ethical blind spots often occur when decision-makers fail to consider different perspectives. This creates particular risk with systems that may impact diverse populations differently. Incorporating diverse stakeholder perspectives provides ethical insight that technical evaluation alone can't deliver.

Financial services firm JPMorgan Chase demonstrates this approach. For high-impact automated decision systems, they convene "perspective panels" with representatives from diverse backgrounds both inside and outside the organisation. These panels systematically consider how different stakeholders might experience the technology application, identifying potential concerns that developers or business sponsors might miss.

Effective stakeholder input processes include genuinely diverse perspectives rather than token representation. They create psychological safety for raising concerns, even uncomfortable ones. They focus discussions on actual impacts rather than just intentions. They also consider both immediate and long-term consequences of technology use across different contexts.

Ethics Beyond Deployment

Ethical responsibility doesn't end when a system is deployed. Many ethical issues emerge only over time as systems operate in real-world conditions, interact with users, and encounter scenarios not anticipated during development.

The healthcare organisation, Cleveland Clinic, illustrates this approach. For their diagnostic support tools, they established ongoing monitoring that tracks not just accuracy metrics but patterns that might indicate ethical concerns. Their system examines whether recommendation acceptance rates differ across patient demographics, if override patterns suggest potential bias, and whether there are unexpected changes in treatment patterns associated with automated recommendations.

Practical continuous monitoring approaches rely on looking beyond technical performance to real-world impacts. They establish clear thresholds for when additional review or intervention is needed. They include both quantitative metrics and qualitative feedback from users and affected stakeholders.

Beyond the Rubber Stamp

Many organisations have established technology ethics committees, but their effectiveness varies widely. According to a recent survey by PwC, 62% of large companies reported having technology ethics committees, but only a third said these committees had substantively changed any decisions, suggesting that many ethics committees function as rubber stamps rather than meaningful governance bodies.

The most effective ethics committees have clear authority and scope—they know exactly what decisions they're responsible for reviewing and what authority they have to recommend changes. They include diverse membership beyond technical specialists, bringing multiple perspectives to ethical evaluations. They integrate with development processes rather than conducting after-the-fact reviews when changes become more complex and costly.

Salesforce provides an instructive example of effective ethics governance. Their Office of Ethical and Humane Use of Technology includes both an internal team and an external advisory council with clear authority to review applications and recommend changes or restrictions. What makes their approach particularly effective is its integration with product development processes—ethical review occurs alongside technical development rather than after completion.

Moving Forward

Ethics discussions can quickly become abstract and disconnected from business realities. Effective ethics requires moving beyond talk to concrete action that shapes how technology is designed, used, and monitored.

"The biggest mistake organisations will make is not thinking of what is guiding this change," Geeta Malhotra observes. This insight highlights the need for explicit ethical frameworks that guide technology development and use. Without these frameworks, ethical considerations remain ad hoc and inconsistent.

Moving from principles to practice requires several key elements working together as a system. Organisations need clear ethical boundaries integrated into their technology strategy from the beginning, not added as an afterthought. They need practical assessment frameworks for evaluating different application types based on potential impact. They must incorporate diverse perspectives in ethical evaluation processes to identify blind spots. Ongoing monitoring beyond initial deployment is essential as systems interact with the real world. Finally, clear accountability for addressing ethical concerns ensures that identified issues lead to actual improvements rather than merely documentation.

The organisations making the most progress on ethics don't treat it as a separate initiative from their core technology strategy. They integrate ethical considerations into every stage of development and use, from initial concept through development, deployment, and ongoing operation. This integration makes ethics a practical part of how technology works rather than a theoretical overlay.

As technology advances, the ethical dimensions of leadership will only grow in importance. The technical complexity may increase, but the fundamental questions remain human ones. What values should guide our use of these powerful tools? What responsibilities do we have to those affected by our decisions? How do we balance innovation with appropriate caution?

Answering these questions will shape your technology strategy and your organisation's relationship with employees, customers, and society. They're not questions you can delegate to technical teams or address through compliance alone. They require leadership judgement informed by diverse perspectives and a clear sense of organisational purpose.

Chapter 6

THE SUSTAINABILITY IMPERATIVE

As his team confronted a practical dilemma, Sundar Pichai, CEO of Google remarked, "We all share a planet. I think that's true for AI." The company's AI systems were delivering clear environmental benefits—cutting data centre energy use by 30% and creating tools to predict wildfire risks, giving communities valuable preparation time. Yet these same AI systems were using concerning amounts of resources: millions of litres of water for cooling and enough electricity per server to power an entire household.

This wasn't merely a technical problem but a leadership challenge relevant to executives across industries. As Google's sustainability team realised that each efficiency improvement was being outpaced by expanding projects, senior leaders faced a straightforward question: should they reduce their AI ambitions, or find a better way to address the resource problem?

"AI is both a powerful tool for environmental conservation and a contributor to our carbon footprint," Pichai noted. "Understanding this relationship is essential for making informed decisions in our increasingly AI-driven world."

Google's experience isn't unique. In boardrooms worldwide, leaders are facing an uncomfortable reality: the very AI technologies that promise remarkable business results are also creating significant environmental challenges. This dual nature of AI, as both an environmental problem and solution, creates a practical leadership challenge that few anticipated.

For Google, the way forward wasn't giving up on AI but rethinking how they implemented it. They couldn't simply halt their AI work—that would surrender competitive advantage and abandon genuine sustainability benefits. But they couldn't ignore the environmental impact either. They needed a practical middle path.

This middle path—using AI in environmentally responsible ways—has become one of the key leadership challenges today. It requires balancing business results with resource responsibility in ways that create advantages rather than compromises. And as we'll see, leaders who tackle this challenge effectively are finding that resource constraints often drive more intelligent, efficient, and ultimately more valuable AI implementations.

The Hidden Environmental Cost of AI

When ChatGPT launched in late 2022, it marked both the beginning of widespread AI adoption and a significant environmental challenge. Behind the simple chat interface lay data centres using electricity at industrial levels. As these AI systems have grown more capable and widely used, their environmental impact has increased accordingly.

Most business leaders don't realise just how resource-intensive these AI systems are. A single large language model training session can produce the carbon equivalent of five cars driven for their entire lifespan—and that's just the training. Daily usage adds considerably more to the environmental footprint.

The figures are concerning. AI systems now account for around 3.7% of global electricity consumption, up from just 1.5% in 2022. If current trends continue, this could reach 10% by 2030—a level that would exceed the entire electricity usage of countries like the UK or Germany.

But carbon emissions aren't the only environmental impact. Water usage presents another substantial challenge. Data centres running AI systems need enormous amounts of water for cooling, particularly as AI processing generates intense heat. These facilities are becoming significant water users, worsening scarcity in many regions where they operate.

Electronic waste adds yet another environmental concern as organisations regularly update their AI hardware. The computing requirements of modern AI systems often need specialised equipment with relatively short useful lives. This creates a disposal problem that compounds with each hardware refresh cycle.

What makes this situation particularly challenging is how invisible these environmental costs remain to most leaders. The clean, digital nature of AI creates an illusion of environmental neutrality that masks its physical resource demands. When we type a prompt into ChatGPT or similar systems, we don't see the thousands of servers, cooling systems, and power supplies working in the background. This disconnect makes it easier to overlook the very real environmental consequences of our AI decisions.

Microsoft's Underwater Solution: Project Natick

This combination of environmental challenges inspired one of the most interesting experiments in computing sustainability: Microsoft's Project Natick.

The idea was both simple and bold—what if we put a data centre at the bottom of the ocean? The concept wasn't mere whimsy but rooted in practical considerations. The sea offers naturally cool temperatures that could eliminate energy-intensive cooling systems. Offshore renewable energy could power the facility. And a sealed environment might protect hardware from the physical disturbances that cause failures on land.

In 2018, Microsoft's team sealed 864 servers—enough to power thousands of AI workloads—into a submarine-like cylinder and sank it 117 feet below the surface near Scotland's Orkney Islands. The data centre operated continuously on the seafloor for two full years.

The results proved remarkably positive. The underwater data centre had a failure rate just one-eighth of traditional land-based facilities. The consistently cool sea temperature eliminated the need for artificial cooling, while the sealed environment protected components from oxygen and humidity, dramatically reducing corrosion.

Perhaps most importantly, the facility ran entirely on locally produced renewable energy from Orkney's wind and solar grid, which is one of the greenest in the world. When the team retrieved the cylinder in 2020, they found the servers inside still working perfectly.

Ben Cutler, who led the project, noted that "Project Natick demonstrated that we could fundamentally rethink data centre design around environmental constraints. Rather than treating sustainability as an afterthought, we made it central to the design process."

The experiment yielded significant insights that continue to influence Microsoft's data centre strategy, with direct applications for reducing the environmental impact of AI computing. It showed that sometimes the most effective environmental solutions aren't incremental improvements to existing approaches, but complete reimaginations of how we solve problems.

The Microsoft case highlights an important principle for sustainable AI: constraints often drive innovation. By accepting the limitations of our planet's resources and designing within those constraints, we can often discover approaches that are not just more sustainable but also more resilient and efficient.

AI's Dual Role

The Microsoft experiment highlights a fascinating paradox in the AI sustainability story: the same technologies creating environmental challenges can help solve them. This dual nature of AI creates both responsibility and opportunity for leaders making technology decisions.

Using AI to Solve AI's Problems

Google's work on data centre optimisation provides a compelling example of this duality. Their team developed an AI system that learned how to control cooling systems more efficiently than human operators could manage. The system predicts future cooling needs based on multiple factors—server load, weather patterns, and time of day—and makes adjustments proactively rather than reactively.

The results were impressive: a 40% reduction in energy used for cooling, translating to a 15% reduction in overall power consumption. The system effectively paid for itself in energy savings while reducing Google's carbon footprint. By 2024, Google had extended this approach across all its commercial data centres globally, achieving a 25% efficiency improvement over previous systems.

This case illustrates AI solving its own problem—the environmental challenge created by AI computation being partially mitigated by AI-driven efficiency. It's an approach that can be applied well beyond data centres.

Supply chain optimisation represents another high-impact application. IBM's work with shipping company Maersk demonstrates how AI can improve supply chain transparency, allowing more accurate emissions accounting and route optimisation. This approach helped Maersk reduce carbon emissions per container transported by 12%.

Even in agriculture, AI applications are optimising resource use and reducing waste. PepsiCo uses AI for precise harvesting and weather forecasting to minimise environmental impact while improving crop yields.

These examples demonstrate that AI's resource consumption shouldn't be evaluated in isolation but in the context of the efficiencies it creates elsewhere. A resource-intensive AI system that significantly reduces waste, energy usage, or emissions in other processes may create a net positive environmental impact despite its own footprint.

For leaders, this suggests a more nuanced approach to AI sustainability than simply minimising computational resources. The key question isn't just "How much does this AI system consume?" but "What is the net environmental impact when considering both the resources used and the efficiencies gained?"

The Geopolitical Wild Card

The sustainability challenges of AI are being further complicated by dramatic changes in geopolitics. As we write this in spring 2025, international trade tensions, national security concerns, and technological sovereignty movements are reshaping how and where AI infrastructure is deployed, with significant implications for environmental impact.

The End of Global AI Infrastructure

For most of the past decade, organisations could deploy AI workloads through globally distributed cloud providers with little concern for national boundaries. That era appears to be ending as technology blocs with diverging standards, supply chains, and regulatory frameworks emerge.

For global organisations, these geopolitical tensions create complex sustainability challenges. Many now face the prospect of maintaining multiple AI infrastructures across different jurisdictions, each with its own environmental footprint. This represents a significant change from the cloud-first, globally centralised approaches that previously dominated.

"We've had to completely rethink our AI infrastructure strategy," shares one of the CTOs of a multinational consumer goods company that we spoke to. "Three years ago, we had a single global AI platform. Now we essentially maintain three separate systems to comply with regional data sovereignty requirements. It's tripled both our costs and our environmental footprint."

The Surprising Return to On-Premises

After a decade-long shift toward cloud computing, geopolitical tensions and data sovereignty concerns are driving a partial reversal—with significant implications for AI sustainability that many leaders haven't fully considered.

"The pendulum is swinging back toward on-premises AI infrastructure, particularly in Europe and parts of Asia," notes technology analyst Maria Korolov. "What most organisations don't realise is that this shift typically increases their carbon footprint substantially."

This sustainability gap exists because cloud providers typically achieve much higher resource utilisation rates and energy efficiency than individual corporate data centres. A typical enterprise data centre might run at 15-25% capacity utilisation, while cloud providers operate at 65-85%—a dramatic efficiency difference.

The on-premises trend is particularly pronounced in regulated industries and regions with strong data sovereignty requirements. For leaders in these sectors, sustainability now requires explicit strategies to mitigate the environmental impact of more localised AI infrastructure.

The Sustainable AI Playbook

Given these substantial environmental considerations, how can leaders deploy AI capabilities while minimising environmental impact? Several approaches have emerged that allow organisations to balance innovation imperatives with sustainability goals.

Doing More with Less

The most direct approach to reducing AI's environmental footprint is using more efficient model architectures and deployment patterns. Recent innovations demonstrate that AI capabilities don't necessarily require ever-increasing computational resources.

"The assumption that bigger models are always better is simply wrong," argues Dr. Wellby. "Many organisations are discovering that smaller, more focussed models often outperform larger ones for specific tasks while consuming a fraction of the resources."

Techniques like model distillation and retrieval-augmented generation (RAG) significantly reduce computational requirements without sacrificing performance. Early research indicates that these methods might cut computational needs by 50-80% while retaining most capabilities.

Domain-specific models present another efficiency opportunity. Rather than using general-purpose foundation models for all tasks, organisations can deploy smaller, specialised models for specific domains. These models, with a fraction of the parameters of general-purpose models, can achieve equal or better performance within their specialisation areas.

The key insight from these approaches is that raw model size isn't the primary determinant of AI capability. For leaders, this means questioning the assumption that bigger models are always better and instead focusing on the right tool for the specific task.

Working with the Sun

Beyond model efficiency, organisations can significantly reduce AI's carbon footprint by aligning computation with renewable energy availability. This approach, known as carbon-aware computing, schedules flexible AI workloads to times and locations with low-carbon electricity.

"Much AI work doesn't need to happen at a specific moment," explains James Hamilton, who leads sustainable infrastructure initiatives at a major cloud provider. "If you can shift training jobs to run when solar or wind generation is high, you can dramatically reduce your carbon footprint without any performance compromise."

Google's implementation of carbon-aware computing reduced the carbon footprint of their flexible computing workloads by 40% without extending completion times (Google, 2022). The approach takes advantage of the inherent flexibility in many AI workflows, particularly training and batch processing.

The natural alignment between flexible workloads and variable renewable energy makes carbon-aware computing particularly valuable for AI. Many AI training and batch inference tasks don't require immediate execution, creating opportunities to schedule them during periods of renewable energy abundance.

Collaborative Infrastructure

The sustainability case for shared AI infrastructure is compelling. Typical enterprise AI clusters operate at only 15-25% utilisation, creating substantial inefficiency in both embodied and operational carbon. Shared infrastructure can dramatically improve this utilisation rate.

"We've seen organisations reduce their AI carbon footprint by 60-70% simply by moving from dedicated to shared infrastructure," notes Dr. Wellby. "It's the equivalent of carpooling versus everyone driving their own car—the total environmental impact drops dramatically when resources are shared efficiently."

Cloud-based AI services represent the most common form of infrastructure sharing. Major providers amortise AI hardware across thousands of customers, achieving 65-85% utilisation rates, which translates directly to a reduced environmental footprint per computation.

For organisations requiring on-premises AI due to data sensitivity or sovereignty requirements, internal sharing models can improve sustainability outcomes. Centralised enterprise AI platforms serving multiple business units can significantly improve hardware utilisation compared to siloed departmental deployments.

What will happen in an Autonomous Future?

The shift from passive AI to agentic systems introduces new levels of computational intensity. Agent systems typically require multiple model calls for a single task, creating substantially higher resource demands than traditional AI applications.

"In our early agent implementations, we saw a 3-5× increase in computational requirements compared to passive AI systems," shares the CTO of a financial services firm. "We quickly realised this approach wouldn't scale environmentally or economically."

This increased computation translates directly to environmental impact, suggesting that widespread adoption of AI agents could significantly increase the energy consumption of enterprise AI compared to current patterns. This projection creates both challenges and opportunities for sustainable AI implementation.

Building Efficient Agents

As AI shifts toward agentic systems, architectural choices become even more critical for sustainability. Several approaches show particular promise for reducing the environmental footprint of agent capabilities.

Modular agent designs could offer significant efficiency advantages through task-specific models. This approach leverages the principle that smaller, focused models can often match or exceed the performance of larger general-purpose models within their domains.

"We've rebuilt our agent architecture to use a 'microservices' approach," explains a lead AI engineer at a retail company. "Instead of running everything through a massive foundation model, we use small, specialised models for specific tasks. Our carbon footprint is about 20% of what it would be with a monolithic approach."

Local execution models represent perhaps the most promising approach for sustainable agents. Local execution on devices—effectively edge processing—instead of cloud-based processing could significantly reduce carbon footprints. Research is underway to determine how much, but the suggestion is that organisations can dramatically reduce energy use and data transfer by running smaller, distilled agent models on local devices rather than in cloud data centres.

The key insight from these approaches is that agent capabilities don't necessarily require proportionally larger environmental footprints. The path to more capable agents isn't simply scaling up—it's designing more efficient cognitive architectures.

The AI Sustainability Quadrant

How do you balance business results with environmental responsibility when implementing AI systems? To help structure your thinking, we've developed a straightforward 2x2 framework: the AI Sustainability Quadrant.

This tool assesses AI projects based on two practical questions:

- ***Business Impact:*** What value does this create for your organisation and stakeholders?
- ***Resource Efficiency:*** How much computing power, energy and water does it use relative to the value created?

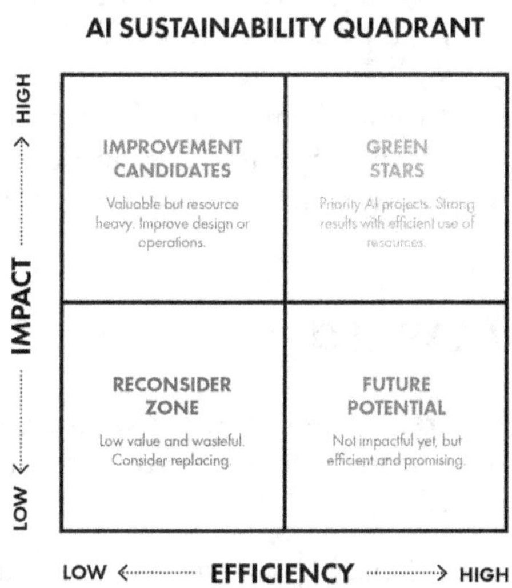

The resulting quadrant creates four categories that help you prioritise and improve your AI work:

- ***Quadrant 1: Green Stars*** (High Impact, High Efficiency) These should be your priority projects—AI applications that deliver substantial business value while using resources efficiently. Examples include smaller, focused models that outperform larger models for specific tasks while using fewer resources.

- ***Quadrant 2: Future Potentials*** (Low Impact, High Efficiency) These projects don't yet deliver significant business results but use resources wisely. They often represent new approaches worth developing further. Small trials using techniques like scheduling workloads during off-peak hours typically fit here.

- ***Quadrant 3: Improvement Candidates*** (High Impact, Low Efficiency) These projects deliver good business results but use too many resources. Rather than scrapping them, focus on keeping their value while improving their efficiency through better design, shared computing resources, or operational changes.

- ***Quadrant 4: Reconsider Zone*** (Low Impact, Low Efficiency) These projects deliver minimal value while using substantial resources and warrant careful review. They often represent "me too" AI investments made without clear purpose or cases where simpler approaches might do the job better.

This framework doesn't suggest eliminating all resource-intensive AI—it helps you make thoughtful choices and identify ways to improve efficiency without sacrificing business value. The goal is balanced decision-making, not rigid categorisation.

Use this quadrant with your team to assess current and planned AI projects, spot improvement opportunities, and ensure your AI work delivers maximum value with minimum environmental impact.

Moving Forward

As a leader, what concrete steps can you take to deploy AI capabilities responsibly? Several priorities emerge from the research and case studies we've examined.

- ***Make AI sustainability measurable***. You can't manage what you don't measure. Organisations that include environmental impact alongside performance and cost metrics in their AI evaluation frameworks achieve significantly better sustainability outcomes. This isn't about creating barriers to AI adoption—it's about making informed choices that consider the full impact of different approaches.

- ***Prioritise AI efficiency*** through architectural choices rather than accepting computational intensity as inevitable. The most sustainable organisations aren't avoiding AI—they're deploying it more intelligently through techniques like retrieval augmentation, distillation, and domain-specific models.

- ***Embrace the potential of shared infrastructure,*** whether through cloud services, internal platforms, or industry collaborations. Improved utilisation rates have substantial environmental benefits, often reducing the carbon footprint of AI

- ***Plan for agentic AI*** by establishing sustainable architectural patterns early. As AI shifts from passive response to active agency, computational demands will increase substantially. Organisations developing efficient agent architectures now will gain competitive and sustainable advantages.

- ***Recognise that sustainable AI isn't just about reducing environmental impact***—it's about creating more value with fewer resources. In a world of constrained computational resources and growing environmental concerns, the most successful AI implementations will be those that maximise impact per unit of energy consumed.

The sustainability imperative in AI isn't separate from business imperatives—it's increasingly aligned with them. As computational resources become more constrained, energy costs rise, and stakeholders demand environmental responsibility, sustainable approaches to AI will become competitive necessities rather than optional considerations.

Ask yourself: How would your AI strategy change if you had to report its carbon footprint to your board? What would happen if you gave Nature a role on your Board? How might AI sustainability metrics influence your technology investment decisions? And most importantly, how can you harness AI's transformative potential while minimising its environmental impact?

The answers to these questions will determine not just the environmental footprint of your AI initiatives, but increasingly their business success as well. The leaders who find the right balance between innovation and sustainability will be those best positioned to thrive in the AI-powered future.

Chapter 7
THE BOARD DYNAMIC

In 2018, the board of HSBC Holdings took a decisive step that few other major companies had attempted. They approved the implementation of an AI system called RAVN to analyse legal documents, automating work that previously required 3,000 hours of legal review time. This wasn't merely a cost-cutting measure; it represented a fundamental shift in how the board approached technology governance. The directors had to trust a system they couldn't fully comprehend to perform critical legal analysis—an area where mistakes could have serious regulatory consequences.

This decision culminated in a year-long process in which HSBC's board systematically built its collective AI literacy through structured education sessions and careful evaluation protocols. The board's chair at the time, Mark Tucker, had insisted that directors understand enough about the technology to evaluate its strategic implications and risk profile, even if they couldn't assess the technical details directly.

"In the past, the board would hear updates about technology during our strategy discussions. Now, we're expected to make significant decisions about capabilities we can barely explain. It's quite humbling," confessed a FTSE 100 board member in our research interviews, capturing the sentiment echoed in boardrooms worldwide as directors confront a governance paradox: how to effectively oversee AI systems they often don't fully comprehend.

Most directors have built distinguished careers mastering complex business challenges, yet now find themselves reliant on others' expertise in areas central to their organisations' future. "One of the boards I sat on had really diverse backgrounds, yet I was the only one thinking that AI is not on the agenda, and shouldn't it be?" reflects Marianne Culver, highlighting how even boards with otherwise strong capabilities often fail to prioritise AI governance appropriately.

The boardroom AI challenge isn't merely theoretical—it has material consequences. Research by the MIT Sloan Management Review shows that insufficient board-level AI oversight has contributed to significant AI mishaps, creating substantial financial and reputational damage. The boards that rise to this challenge will enable their organisations to harness AI's potential while mitigating risks; those that don't may find themselves accountable for failures they didn't see coming.

The Boardroom Expertise Gap

During our research, we examined the background and experience of all chairs and non-executive directors (NEDs) across the UK's FTSE 100. The findings were sobering: only eight chairs had proven AI or technology leadership experience. Among approximately 800 NEDs, only 48 came from technology functions, had significant technology company experience, or were explicitly recruited as digital NEDs.

This representation gap explains why many boards struggle with effective AI oversight. When fewer than 6% of board members have meaningful technology expertise, boards inevitably face challenges in evaluating AI strategies and risks. This expertise deficit creates a fundamental governance dilemma: How can boards fulfil their oversight responsibilities when they lack the knowledge to evaluate proposals critically?

Our interviews with board members across multiple sectors found a common pattern: boards often delegate AI oversight to traditional IT leaders who may lack a broader digital and AI perspective. This delegation reflects a fundamental misunderstanding of AI's strategic nature. While IT has traditionally been considered an operational function, AI represents a strategic capability that touches every aspect of the business, from customer experience to risk management to talent strategy.

The traditional approach of appointing a single "digital director" proves increasingly insufficient. As Microsoft's board discovered when implementing its responsible AI framework in 2019, digital expertise can't be delegated to a single board member; it needs to be developed collectively because governance decisions about AI touch every aspect of the business.

Leading Through the Rear-View Mirror

Although we are not suggesting that all board chairs embody what we've termed earlier in the book as "rearview mirror leadership"—applying governance approaches from the past to technologies that operate by fundamentally different rules—it is equally clear that many do. We did find standout examples of Chairs who are really driving the AI strategic agenda in boardroom discussions, and in financial services in particular, we found quite sophisticated AI governance, boardroom maturity, and AI strategy. However, in many we researched, and we suspect many further in the FTS250 and beyond, this backwards-looking mindset is happening in several ways.

Chairs often prioritise risk management over opportunity creation when evaluating AI initiatives. While prudent governance requires risk assessment, overemphasising risk leads boards to approve only incremental AI applications rather than potentially transformative ones.

Many chairs equate governance thoroughness with time invested, assuming that more extended discussions necessarily produce better oversight. But AI governance quality depends more on asking the right questions than on extended deliberation about the wrong ones.

Chairs often select CEOs primarily for operational execution rather than transformative leadership. While operational excellence matters, AI's disruptive potential means boards increasingly need CEOs capable of fundamental business reinvention. When chairs prioritise steady performance over transformation capability in CEO selection, they may inadvertently hamstring their organisations' AI adaptation.

BP's board learned this lesson painfully in April 2025. Chair Helge Lund paid the price of losing investor confidence when a radical strategy that had failed to deliver under Lund and his first transformative CEO, Bernard Looney, was merely reinforced by the incoming CEO, Murray Auchincloss, who had previously been the group CFO. To Lund, this internal appointment was a "safe bet" that showed continuity, and Auchincloss fitted the profile of an operational CEO rather than a transformative one. To many of the employees and stakeholders, it seemed more like Lund was reinforcing failure than really understanding the needs of his key stakeholders. It cost him his job.

The Missing AI Governance Layer

The most concerning pattern we've observed across multiple sectors is the absence of a clear governance layer for AI initiatives. Most boards have established well-defined governance frameworks for financial decisions, major investments, and even cybersecurity. However, AI governance often remains ad hoc, creating potential oversight gaps.

"We make sure in the board meetings that the audit subcommittee, which previously looked at Digital and cyber, has evolved to include AI. We discuss how we set up the [AI] environment, what the checks and balances are, and how we should leverage its potential. It has become part of our standing agenda with the board," explains Guy Moeyens, the CEO of VTTI, a multinational Energy infrastructure company, describing a systematic approach that remains the exception rather than the rule.

This governance gap creates three significant vulnerabilities.

- ***Inconsistent evaluation standards.*** Without structured assessment frameworks, boards evaluate similar AI initiatives differently depending on who presents them or which directors happen to ask questions. This inconsistency undermines objective governance.

- ***Inadequate risk identification.*** Traditional risk frameworks often fail to address AI-specific concerns like algorithmic bias, model drift, or unforeseen emergent behaviours. Without AI-specific risk evaluation, boards may miss critical vulnerabilities.

- ***Insufficient implementation monitoring.*** AI systems evolve over time in ways traditional technologies don't. Boards that treat AI approval as a point-in-time decision rather than establishing ongoing monitoring mechanisms may miss problematic system evolution.

The most effective boards establish clear governance frameworks for AI that specify which AI decisions require board approval, what information the board needs for evaluation, how implementation will be monitored, and which ethical standards apply. These frameworks create governance consistency while acknowledging AI's unique characteristics.

When JPMorgan Chase established their AI and Machine Learning Governance Forum in 2019, it created a structured escalation path for AI decisions that required board-level attention. This approach allowed the board to focus its limited time on the most consequential AI decisions while ensuring consistent evaluation standards across the organisation.

"Sometimes AI is brilliant, and you should treat it as if it has its own seat at the board table. If you get to that point, then I would say, then you are embracing it in a meaningful way. But it should not be that ... because the whole management did an AI seminar ... we are all suddenly smart, while at the same time, you are asking your PA to print your Board papers," advises Christoph Debus, CEO of the German travel giant, DER.

When Directors Don't Challenge Enough

Perhaps the most concerning governance pattern we've observed is an insufficient challenge between non-executive directors and executive teams regarding AI initiatives. This occurs in several ways.

Executive teams often present AI proposals using technical language that non-technical directors struggle to understand. When directors don't know what they're evaluating, meaningful challenges become impossible, regardless of their intentions or diligence.

Non-executive directors often hesitate to ask fundamental questions about AI proposals, fearing they'll appear technologically naive. This hesitation creates a silence that executives interpret as understanding or agreement when it actually reflects confusion or uncertainty.

Many boards lack structured questioning frameworks for AI initiatives, leading to inconsistent and often superficial challenges. Without clear expectations about what directors should probe, challenges depend on individual directors' confidence and knowledge rather than systematic governance approaches.

Board dynamics around AI will vary dramatically across sectors. Marco Wirén, who became the Vice-Chairman of Nesté, found himself in an unusual position when he joined. He alone seemed to have tangible experience with AI, so he decided to push the AI agenda forward at the board level gently. Fast forward five years, and AI is not just a regular touchpoint in their board meetings, but most of his former board colleagues now have real experience of AI in a strategic context.

While most boards have progressed from complete AI unawareness to at least recognising their knowledge gaps –few have genuine AI expertise in the boardroom. The exceptions tend to be highly regulated or technology-driven organisations, where directors bring substantive AI experience to the table. In most cases, though, there's still a significant AI capability gap at the very top.

"On the board, I became known as the 'AI Agent provocateur'. I built a good rapport with the chair, who valued the perspective. My approach was simple: keep putting AI on the agenda and challenge the executive team with questions like 'Could we move faster here?' or 'What if we thought bigger about this?' I was always pushing them to explore applications they hadn't considered before. Someone on every Board needs to play that role."

Starbucks experienced this challenge when implementing its Deep Brew AI initiative in 2019. Initial board discussions focused extensively on technical aspects while overlooking key strategic questions about how the technology would change customer relationships. Only after establishing a structured questioning framework did the board begin evaluating the initiative's strategic implications effectively.

When boards don't understand what they're approving, they can't exercise genuine oversight, regardless of their intentions or diligence. Clear communication enables meaningful governance despite asymmetric expertise.

Effective translation requires effort from both directors and technical leaders. Directors must develop sufficient vocabulary to engage with key concepts, while technical teams must learn to communicate without jargon or unnecessary complexity. This mutual adaptation enhances governance effectiveness by creating shared understanding of critical issues. The book "51 Key AI Terms Explained for Leaders", written by one of the authors, is designed to meet this need specifically. It provides a precise formal definition, a simplified version in "real English", and a case study that brings the term and the context to life. We thoroughly recommend that you give a copy to each of your Board directors as a reference tool and in an effort to help them raise their dQ. The QR Code for the link to the book is given at the very end of this book.

AI's Unique Governance Challenges

AI isn't just another technology requiring oversight—it introduces qualitatively different governance challenges that traditional approaches often fail to address:

AI systems can make consequential decisions autonomously. Unlike traditional technologies that execute explicit instructions, AI systems make judgments based on patterns they've identified. This autonomous decision-making creates governance challenges that traditional oversight mechanisms weren't designed to address. If a hard stop or abort option isn't clear without compromising business continuity, checks and balances haven't been appropriately built in.

AI systems evolve over time through continued learning. A system that meets all governance requirements at implementation may evolve in ways that later create risks. This evolution requires ongoing oversight rather than point-in-time approval, challenging traditional governance models.

AI failures can affect thousands or millions of stakeholders simultaneously. The scale and speed of potential harm create risk profiles unlike those of most traditional technologies. When autonomous systems make decisions across large populations, failures can scale catastrophically before human intervention.

Third-party AI components create complex accountability challenges. Most organisations rely on external AI components they didn't develop and don't fully understand. Yet boards remain accountable for outcomes regardless of whether AI systems are developed internally or externally.

These characteristics demand new governance approaches. Traditional risk frameworks organised around security, privacy, and compliance often fail to address AI's unique aspects like algorithmic bias, autonomous decision-making, or emergent behaviours.

The Third-Party AI Challenge

The governance challenge extends beyond internally developed AI to the complex mesh, in jargon called an 'ecosystem', of vendors, partners, and third-party systems on which most organisations rely. The average large organisation uses AI components from numerous vendors, creating significant governance complexity.

This complexity introduces new accountability challenges. A 2023 study by Gartner found that 73% of major AI failures involve third-party components, yet in most cases, boards devote minimal attention to third-party AI governance. This oversight gap represents a significant governance vulnerability.

The legal implications are equally concerning. Organisations can't shield themselves from liability by attributing failures to third-party AI components. Boards remain accountable for outcomes regardless of whether AI systems are developed internally or externally.

Leading boards are developing more robust governance approaches for third-party AI by requiring enhanced due diligence protocols. These practices include vendor assessment frameworks specific to AI, contractual provisions addressing algorithmic accountability, and ongoing monitoring mechanisms for third-party AI systems.

Goldman Sachs' board implemented a structured third-party AI governance framework in 2021 that requires enhanced due diligence for any external AI components used in client-facing applications. This approach has enabled more effective oversight of their extended AI ecosystem while maintaining the firm's ability to innovate quickly.

These approaches acknowledge that governing third-party AI requires more than traditional vendor management. It requires a structured evaluation of algorithmic governance practices, data usage policies, and ethical frameworks—areas that traditional procurement processes rarely address adequately. By developing AI-specific vendor governance protocols, boards can effectively oversee their extended AI ecosystems more effectively.

Preparing for AI Crises

The potential for AI systems to create unexpected crises presents another governance challenge. Major AI-related corporate crises range from algorithmic discrimination incidents to automated systems making catastrophic decisions at scale. These incidents cause substantial financial and reputational damage.

When Microsoft's Tay chatbot began posting offensive content in 2016 after learning from malicious user inputs, the company faced a significant crisis that required immediate board attention. Despite having strong technical capabilities, Microsoft's board at the time lacked specific AI crisis protocols, which hampered their initial response.

Despite this risk, board preparedness for AI crises remains limited. While most boards have discussed specific crisis response protocols for cybersecurity incidents and financial irregularities, far fewer have done the same for AI failures. This preparedness gap creates significant vulnerability.

The speed and scale of AI crises demand particular preparedness. Algorithmic failures can affect thousands or millions of stakeholders simultaneously, while the technical complexity often hampers quick response. Traditional crisis management assumes you understand what went wrong, but with complex AI systems, determining the cause can take days while the crisis unfolds in hours.

Forward-thinking boards are developing AI-specific crisis protocols that address these unique challenges. These typically include technical response teams with the authority to suspend automated systems, enhanced monitoring for early detection of algorithmic anomalies, and communication strategies that address the unique aspects of AI incidents. These preparations enhance organisational resilience against the distinctive crisis patterns that AI can create.

Perhaps most importantly, effective crisis planning includes governance provisions that clarify board roles during AI incidents. Boards with clearly defined crisis protocols intervene more effectively during incidents, providing strategic guidance without hampering operational response. This clarity is particularly valuable during the confusion that often accompanies AI failures.

Building the Board's AI Confidence

The governance challenges outlined above might seem daunting, particularly for boards with limited technical expertise. However, effective AI governance doesn't require boards to become technical experts—it requires them to develop specific capabilities that enable informed oversight despite limited expertise.

We've identified six domains of AI literacy that enable effective board oversight without requiring technical expertise:

Strategic literacy

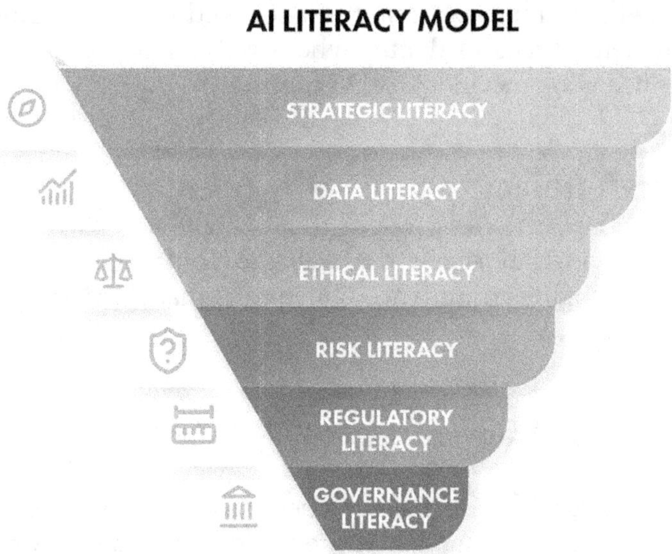

Involves understanding AI's potential impacts on business models, competitive dynamics, and organisational capabilities. This domain connects AI to familiar strategic considerations, enabling directors to evaluate initiatives against business objectives.

Data literacy

Focuses on understanding how data quality affects AI outcomes. This domain helps directors identify critical questions about data sources and potential biases without requiring technical knowledge about algorithms.

Ethical Literacy

Addresses the distinct ethical implications of automated decision systems. This domain enables directors to evaluate the ethical dimensions of AI deployments, an increasingly important governance responsibility.

Risk Literacy

Encompasses the unique risk patterns associated with AI deployment. This domain helps directors identify where traditional risk management approaches need enhancement for AI contexts.

Regulatory Literacy

Covers the evolving landscape of AI-specific regulations. This domain helps boards navigate compliance obligations that increasingly affect AI deployments.

Governance Literacy

Addresses the oversight mechanisms needed for responsible AI. This domain helps directors establish appropriate governance frameworks without requiring detailed technical understanding.

"On the Engineering Company Main Board that I sit on, we've taken a more radical approach to the impact of AI. As a team, we have high strategic AI and Risk literacy. We have agreed that AI will massively disrupt the current business model," explains Mikko Tepponen. "...So we set ourselves some ambitious goals; already in 3 years, we have gone from 2% AI-enabled engineering work to 35. And even some of that's the discussion in the Board, whether that's ambitious enough for the people in the company."

These literacy domains focus on what directors need to know rather than attempting to replicate technical expertise. By developing these targeted competencies, boards can exercise effective oversight while acknowledging the boundaries of their expertise.

Creating Collective AI Competence

Beyond individual director development, leading organisations are implementing structured learning journeys that build collective board competence. We've found that coordinated learning experiences produce better governance outcomes than individual development alone.

These collective learning journeys typically combine formal education, experiential elements, and reflective discussions. Formal components might include expert briefings or structured courses, while experiential elements often involve demonstrations of AI applications or discussions with implementation teams. Reflective discussions then connect these experiences to governance responsibilities.

"One of the things we've also invited the board to do, given our own Exco experience, which was so eye-opening and successful, is to take the board to this lab with PWC", notes Guy Moeyens.

The most effective learning journeys are tailored to directors' existing knowledge and governance responsibilities rather than providing generic technical education. Board development should focus on governance implications rather than technical details, helping directors understand enough to govern effectively without attempting to make them technical experts.

Time constraints make efficiency essential in these learning journeys. Directors typically allocate only limited hours annually to technology-specific board development despite rating it as highly important. This limited time must be used strategically to build the most critical competencies.

Unilever's board implemented a structured AI learning journey in 2020 that combined formal education, practical demonstrations, and governance discussions. Rather than attempting to make directors technical experts, the program focused on building specific governance capabilities relevant to their oversight responsibilities. This targeted approach enabled more effective governance while respecting directors' limited time availability.

Importantly, effective learning journeys extend beyond technical topics to include ethical, social, and regulatory dimensions of AI governance. These aspects are often more directly relevant to board responsibilities than technical details, yet receive proportionally less attention in many board development programs. Comprehensive learning journeys address this imbalance by covering the full spectrum of governance considerations.

Asking the Right Questions

For many directors, the most practical approach to AI governance lies in asking the right questions rather than attempting to evaluate technical details directly. We've identified four categories of questions that enable effective oversight:

- Strategic questions evaluate alignment with organisational objectives:
    - How does this AI initiative support our strategy?
    - What advantage will it create?
    - How will we measure success?
- Implementation questions address execution capabilities:
    - Do we have the necessary talent and data?
    - Have we evaluated make-versus-buy decisions appropriately?
    - What timeline assumptions underlie the proposal?
- Risk questions identify potential downsides:
    - What are the primary failure modes?
    - How might this system create unintended consequences?
    - What monitoring will detect problems early?
- Ethical questions address broader implications:
    - How might this system affect different stakeholders?
    - What values are implicitly encoded in design choices?
    - How transparent should our approach be?

This questioning framework enables directors to exercise meaningful oversight without requiring detailed technical knowledge. The right questions create accountability and surface critical issues without requiring boards to evaluate technical details directly. This approach acknowledges the asymmetry of expertise while maintaining robust governance.

Netflix's board adopted a structured questioning framework for AI initiatives in 2021 that ensures consistent evaluation across different proposals. This framework has enabled more effective governance by providing a shared language for discussing AI initiatives while clarifying what information directors need for evaluation.

Leading boards are formalising these questioning frameworks into structured evaluation protocols for AI initiatives. These protocols ensure the consistent application of oversight principles while providing management with clear expectations about what information boards require. This structured approach enhances governance effectiveness while respecting the boundaries between oversight and operations.

Moving Forward

The challenges outlined in this chapter represent what we call the "AI governance paradox"—boards must govern technologies they don't fully understand. This paradox creates legitimate anxiety because directors are accountable for decisions they can't fully evaluate independently.

But the governance paradox isn't unique to AI—it's an intensified version of challenges boards have faced before. Few directors have deep expertise in all aspects of their oversight responsibilities, whether finance, operations, human resources, or marketing. Effective governance has always required structured approaches that enable oversight despite limited expertise.

The path forward lies in five key actions:

- *Acknowledge the governance gap:* Accept that board members won't become AI technical experts but can develop sufficient literacy to provide meaningful oversight.

- *Focus on governance capabilities:* Develop sufficient literacy to ask the right questions, evaluate proposed approaches, and recognise warning signs.

- *Establish clear boundaries:* Distinguish between technical decisions requiring management expertise and strategic or ethical decisions requiring board involvement.

- *Create structured frameworks:* Implement consistent questioning frameworks that enable meaningful oversight without requiring technical expertise.

- ***Integrate AI governance:*** Incorporate AI oversight into existing board structures rather than treating it as an isolated technical matter.

The most effective boards will not have the deepest technical expertise—they will develop systematic approaches that enable meaningful oversight despite asymmetric knowledge. The governance paradox can't be eliminated, but with structured approaches, it can be navigated successfully.

As you consider your board's AI readiness, ask yourself: How clearly have you defined the boundaries between technical decisions and governance matters requiring board involvement? What structured approaches might enable more effective oversight despite limited expertise? The answers to these questions will shape your board's readiness for the governance challenges ahead.

Chapter 8

THE C-SUITE CHALLENGE

When Unilever embarked on its digital transformation journey in 2017, CEO Paul Polman faced a critical leadership challenge. The consumer goods giant sought to modernise its approach to everything from supply chain management to marketing analytics using artificial intelligence and advanced data systems. Yet within Unilever's C-suite, dramatically different perspectives emerged about how aggressively to pursue these technological changes.

Keith Weed, then Chief Marketing Officer, pushed for rapid adoption of AI-powered consumer analytics to personalise marketing across Unilever's vast portfolio of brands. Graeme Pitkethly, CFO, expressed concern about the substantial investments required without clear short-term returns. Leena Nair, CHRO at the time, raised questions about workforce implications and the potential for skills gaps across the company's global operations.

As documented in Unilever's 2018 Annual Report and later analysed in a 2020 INSEAD case study titled "Unilever's Digital Transformation," Polman recognised that these divergent viewpoints weren't merely philosophical disagreements—they represented fundamentally different risk assessments, investment priorities, and implementation timelines that could derail the company's digital ambitions. Yet there was an urgency to them that could not be ignored.

Rather than allowing these differences to create strategic paralysis, Polman implemented what the company called its "Connected 4 Growth" organisational design. This approach explicitly acknowledged different functional perspectives while creating a shared decision framework and cross-functional teams that balanced ambitious digital goals with business discipline. The results were significant: between 2017 and 2022, Unilever's digitally-enabled brands grew 69% faster than the rest of the portfolio, and AI-powered supply chain improvements delivered over €500 million in savings, according to the company's 2022 financial statements.

Many executives feel this underlying sense of urgency as they confront AI's impact on their business. "This is going so fast that we can miss the train if we don't try to educate ourselves first and see what we can do as a company," observes Guy Moeyens, CEO of VTTI.

If you step into most C-suites today, you'll find a striking reality: leaders aren't even having the same conversation. While one executive sees an existential competitive threat, another sees budget-reduction priorities. Where the CTO envisions transformative potential, the CFO sees unproven investments with questionable returns.

These nuanced and diverging perspectives create a leadership paradox. The very technologies demanding a unified strategic direction are the ones that are dramatically splitting apart the different executive viewpoints. This isn't merely a philosophical disagreement—it directly impacts execution speed, investment decisions, and, ultimately, competitive position.

This chapter examines why C-Suite perspectives naturally diverge when confronting these technologies, how these differences create strategic vulnerability, and what approaches create alignment without requiring everyone to become technical experts. If you're not in the C-Suite, this will help you understand your leaders' perspectives.

If you are in the C-Suite, we hope this will help you reflect on why alignment with your peers is essential for effective AI leadership.

Why Leadership Teams Disagree About AI

The divergent viewpoints emerging in leadership teams aren't primarily personality conflicts or individual resistance. They stem from structural factors that create predictable tension: functional priorities, incentive structures, professional backgrounds, and varying exposure to technological possibilities. These dynamics result in a natural divergence, particularly around emerging technologies that challenge the status quo.

McKinsey's 2022 research on leadership alignment during digital transformations reveals that organisations with aligned leadership teams are 2.3 times more likely to report successful digital initiatives than those with significant executive misalignment. This research, published in their "Digital Transformation: Making it Work" report, underscores how critical it is to address the structural drivers that create fault lines in how executives approach transformation decisions.

Adobe's successful transition to a cloud-based business model provides a compelling example of leadership alignment in action. When CEO Shantanu Narayen faced the challenge of shifting from traditional software sales to subscription services—a move with profound implications for revenue recognition, customer relationships, operating model and technology infrastructure—Adobe's leadership team deliberately created cross-functional integration mechanisms. This approach transformed what could have been technological fragmentation into a coherent strategy that ultimately tripled Adobe's valuation between 2013 and 2018, according to their annual reports and Harvard Business Review's 2019 case study "Adobe's Software Transformation."

Different Roles, Different Priorities

Each C-suite function sees AI differently, creating natural tension about priorities that must be understood to create alignment.

The CEO

CEOs typically focus on strategic delivery and competitive implications. Their orientation toward market position and strategic advantage creates natural impatience with technical constraints that slow deployment. "I remember being very frustrated that our legacy technology was holding back our ability to deploy a new app that customers were crying out for," noted one CEO we spoke with, capturing the competitive pressure many chief executives feel.

This sense of 'pace versus readiness' is one of the typical concerns CEOs have over AI's potential; their concerns are broader than those of other organisational leaders. Many CEOs are genuinely concerned about losing their grip on consistency, accountability, and risk management. The degree to which they will genuinely lead on AI or be a fast follower will reflect their digital maturity.

We see more and more CEOs who understand the potential of digital, particularly in consumer-facing sectors such as telecommunications, retail, banking, and FMCG. This is less true in manufacturing, industrial, and other B2B businesses. CEOs have often come up through Finance or Operations functions and still have that operational or "quarterly" focus as a default. Their digital intelligence (dQ) is usually lower than it should be for such a strategic role, leading many organisations to hire Chief Digital Officers to help transform the organisation.

Another executive we interviewed, who sits on the board of a Private Equity business and an FTSE250 company, said that some organisations frame the conversation differently: "In the PE [portfolio] companies, the CEOs board view it more as how AI can help us power the commercial engine... whereas in the other [FTSE250] board it is much more of a risk-biased cyber-focused discussion." This commercial focus can create productive alignment when all executives share it.

The Chief Financial Officer (CFO)

CFOs bring a financial lens that is usually focused on prioritisation and emphasising measurable returns. Where the CEO is judged on vision, the CFO is judged on outcomes. This often creates natural caution about significant, speculative technology investments without clear ROI metrics. Bain & Company's 2023 report "The CFO's Role in Digital

Transformation" highlights this tension, finding that 62% of CFOs cite unclear ROI as their primary concern with AI investments, while only 28% of CTOs rank this as a top issue.

There are exceptions to this pattern. As far back as 2017, Marco Wiren, then CFO of Wärtsilä, the Finnish maritime giant, was the first C-Suite executive to embrace Robotic Process Automation (RPA) and other AI tools in his department. Now, at Nokia as CFO, he still balances his enthusiasm for the opportunity with the need to ensure the investments drive a suitable return. "It is easy to get excited by AI, but when deploying it within a technology company and at scale, we have to be sure of the potential risks and to have confidence in the rate of return it will provide," he explained in our interview.

The CFO's concerns typically fall into four key categories:

- ***Data accuracy and integrity*** - AI relies on high-quality data, and CFOs often know how imperfect corporate data actually is
- ***Audit and compliance risks*** - AI systems that cannot explain their reasoning raise red flags in audits
- ***Legal, regulatory and reputational risks*** - Many of these fall back personally on the CFO
- ***Return on investment*** - Ensuring that AI investments produce measurable financial benefits

Lisa Su's leadership at AMD demonstrates how these tensions can be productively resolved. When rebuilding AMD's competitive position against Intel between 2014 and 2019, Su deliberately created shared metrics combining financial discipline with technological ambition—an approach that allowed AMD to make significant R&D investments while maintaining investor confidence through clear financial guardrails. This balanced approach, documented in Fortune's 2020 profile "How Lisa Su Turned Around AMD," provides a model for aligning financial prudence with technological advancement.

Chief Technical Officer (CTO), Chief Digital Officer(CDO) and Chief Information Officer(CIO)

CTOs, CDOs, and CIOs often bring perspectives on infrastructure, security, and innovation. They usually deal with a tricky balancing act between needing to fix years of under-investment in core enterprise systems, with the opportunity to innovate and create future-resilient solutions that the business and its customers need. They depend on access to the right talent and sufficient capital to run core systems while still investing in the new.

Chief Operations Officer (COO) and P&L Holders

COOs and divisional P&L holders approach AI through a distinctly operational lens, focused on tangible performance improvements and measurable business outcomes. Their perspective is shaped by daily accountability for concrete results and the relentless pressure to deliver against targets. "I need AI to solve real problems today, not promise theoretical benefits tomorrow," explained one consumer goods divisional president of consumer goods we interviewed. Unlike other C-suite members who might evaluate AI more conceptually, these executives seek immediate operational impact – improved productivity, reduced costs, enhanced quality, or accelerated delivery times.

This operational focus creates a practical, results-oriented perspective that can be both an advantage and a limitation. P&L holders tend to embrace AI solutions with a clear, near-term impact on their performance metrics. Unilever's divisional leaders, for example, rapidly adopted AI-powered demand forecasting when they saw it could reduce inventory costs by 15-20% while improving product availability, as documented in their 2022 Supply Chain Innovation Report. However, this same pragmatism can create resistance to more transformative AI applications where benefits are less certain or longer-term.

The most effective divisional leaders balance immediate operational results with longer-term capability building. They recognise that some AI investments deliver quick wins while others build essential foundations for future competitiveness. This balanced perspective is increasingly important as the line between operational and strategic technology blurs. As one division president noted in our research interviews: "The days of separating 'run the business' from 'change the business' are over. Today's operational AI solutions are tomorrow's competitive necessities."

Chief HR Officer or Chief People Officer (CHRO/CPO)

CHROs focus on workforce implications that often receive insufficient attention from other executives. The human dimension of technological change—skills development, job redesign, change management—usually exists at the periphery of strategy discussions until implementation problems emerge. Many HR leaders we interviewed come from traditional HR backgrounds and are often nervous about AI's built-in biases that might cause legal or ethical backlash. They are frequently suspicious of the 'black box' nature of some AI tools and concerned that AI can depersonalise key moments, like feedback or layoffs.

The resulting dysfunction and misalignment aren't surprising. When executives agree about "importance" without aligning on specific priorities, they have entirely different conversations while believing they're aligned. This creates implementation confusion, resource conflicts, and strategy drift that delay effective action.

Speed Versus Safety

Beyond differing priorities, leadership teams often struggle with the pace at which new technologies, particularly AI, should be adopted. Some executives see urgency; others want more clarity before committing. This tension is real and common.

One factor is generational. As Simon Lucas observed in our interview, "Younger colleagues in their twenties and thirties tend to experiment more with AI tools. Senior leaders, often in their fifties or sixties, may be more hesitant." This isn't about capability but familiarity. Korn Ferry's 2023 research "Digital Leadership Dynamics" supports this, showing that age-diverse leadership teams exhibit much broader variance in digital risk appetite.

Mikko Tepponen summarised it well when he told us, "I don't think people are realising how fast it's going to move now." This perception gap can be dangerous. The risk is not just that a company moves too slowly but that it doesn't realise it's being outpaced until it's too late.

There are other reasons behind cautious behaviour. Many executives bear the scars of previous technology projects that exceeded their budgets or delivered underwhelming results. They are wary of enthusiasm becoming overreach. AI, still unfamiliar to many, brings a level of uncertainty that justifies some level of prudence.

That said, delaying AI conversations entirely can carry significant risks. One board member told us that he had suggested a discussion on how AI could impact business strategy—"two years later, the session still hadn't happened." This inertia isn't neutrality; it's a form of passive decision-making with real consequences.

The challenge is to match pace to context. Not all AI initiatives require the same urgency. Customer-facing use cases, where experimentation is relatively low risk, may benefit from quick testing and iteration. Backend infrastructure changes, on the other hand, demand a more measured approach.

Siemens' approach to AI adoption offers a relevant example from outside the technology sector. According to a 2022 case study published by the European Business Review, CEO Roland Busch faced significant internal disagreement about how quickly to integrate AI across the industrial giant's diverse business units after taking over in 2021.

Rather than enforcing a single adoption pace, Busch implemented what Siemens termed their "Digital Enterprise Velocity Framework." As documented in Siemens' 2022 Digital Enterprise Report, this approach created different speeds for different contexts: rapid experimentation for customer-facing applications and predictive maintenance, while maintaining a more measured pace for core industrial systems where safety and reliability were paramount.

This multi-speed approach enabled Siemens to move quickly in areas where competition demanded it, while maintaining appropriate caution in domains where risks were higher. The lesson for leadership teams is to avoid one-size-fits-all mindsets. Some AI applications should move fast. Others shouldn't.

False urgency, often driven by Fear of Missing Out (FOMO), is another issue. Seeing a competitor launch an AI-powered tool or hearing about rapid productivity gains can create pressure to jump in, without enough grounding in what success really looks like. The right response to FOMO is capability building, not copying.

Rapid prototyping tools and low-code/no-code solutions now allow teams to test AI in a controlled way. Building a Minimum Viable Product (MVP) using these platforms can give tangible results quickly, reducing both uncertainty and risk. The smartest leadership teams now use these approaches to shorten decision cycles and increase shared understanding without overcommitting.

Different Views on Risk

Not only do the different roles across the C-suite approach AI from different perspectives, but they also interpret risk in different ways. This is not just about personality or risk aversion. It reflects how incentives and responsibilities are distributed.

Technical leaders tend to focus on performance risk—will the model work at scale? Legal and compliance teams are more attuned to regulatory exposure and explainability. Customer-facing roles prioritise reputational risk—the risk of damaged trust—while finance teams worry about underperformance against budget.

The Economist Intelligence Unit's 2022 report "Digital Risk: C-Suite Perspectives" highlights that these variances are systematic. A survey of 600 global executives found that technical executives typically rate the risk of AI failure 35% lower than their legal and finance colleagues. Without an integrated view of risk, AI projects become battlegrounds rather than cross-functional efforts.

Maersk, the global shipping and logistics company, tackled this challenge head-on during its digital transformation. According to a 2021 case study published in the Journal of Business Strategy, CEO Søren Skou recognised that different executives had fundamentally different risk perceptions about their AI initiatives to optimise shipping routes and container placements.

In response, Maersk developed what they called their "Technology Risk Integration Framework" in 2019. This framework required every major digital initiative to be assessed across multiple dimensions—technical feasibility, customer impact, financial returns, and regulatory compliance. According to Maersk's 2020 Digital Integration Report, this approach didn't eliminate disagreements, but it created a shared process for working through them, accelerating decision-making by 40% for major technology investments.

One cause of misalignment is how technology has historically been treated within organisations—as a cost, not a value driver. Many IT functions still report to Finance, reinforcing the idea that technology should be controlled and contained rather than explored and invested in. This dynamic affects risk tolerance across the board.

As Mark Whiteling asked pointedly in our interview: "Why isn't the failure to embrace technology one of your top ten risks? Is it because you've evaluated it and ruled it out—or because you haven't even asked the question?" That kind of questioning reflects a deeper problem—many leaders still don't see digital fluency as essential to commercial judgment.

Procter & Gamble's experience illustrates how making risk perspectives explicit can transform decision-making. According to a 2021 case study published in the Harvard Business Review titled "P&G's Digital Transformation," CEO David Taylor recognised that different functional leaders had fundamentally different risk perceptions about the company's AI initiatives. Marketing saw opportunity, Finance saw uncertainty, and Legal saw compliance challenges.

In response, P&G developed what they called their "Connected Risk Framework" in 2019. This approach required executives to explicitly state their risk assumptions about AI initiatives and collectively evaluate them. As documented in P&G's 2020 Annual Report, this framework didn't eliminate disagreements but created a shared vocabulary for discussing risk across functions.

The key insight from P&G's experience is that these different risk perspectives aren't wrong; they're incomplete if considered in isolation. A mature approach acknowledges that AI risk isn't one thing. It includes technical failure, business irrelevance, customer backlash, ethical controversy, and regulatory violation. The more balanced your risk model, the stronger your decision-making.

Incentives also shape these positions. Legal and finance leaders often face asymmetric downside risk. If something goes wrong, they take the blame. If it goes well, they don't necessarily get the credit. Product and tech leaders often see the reverse: their reputations rise if it works, but failure is treated as a shared learning experience. These differences make alignment more complicated—but also more important.

When executives make their risk assumptions explicit, decision-making improves. When they don't, fear and optimism fight it out behind closed doors.

When Understanding Varies

The most fundamental tension in many C-suites is not about goals or timelines. It's about understanding. Executives vary widely in how confident they feel discussing AI. That matters more than most realise.

Guy Moeyens noted in our interview that "some board members still take notes on paper. Their companies may be digital leaders, but that doesn't mean the individuals themselves are." McKinsey's 2022 research "Digital Leadership Gaps" shows that teams with a shared baseline of understanding—what we call digital intelligence, or dQ—are more than three times more likely to succeed with technology initiatives.

When knowledge varies too widely, several issues appear. First, information gets filtered. Technical leaders simplify their messages for peers who aren't confident with jargon, thereby losing important nuances. Second, credibility suffers. A non-technical executive may struggle to judge whether a proposed solution is credible or just fashionable. Third, communication breaks down. Many business priorities have no precise technical equivalent, and vice versa.

Nestlé tackled this challenge during their digital transformation between 2018 and 2021. According to a 2022 case study published by IMD Business School, CEO Mark Schneider recognised that different executives needed different levels of digital knowledge. Rather than expecting everyone to become technical experts, Nestlé developed what they called "Digital Foundations" – a tiered learning approach tailored to executives' roles and responsibilities.

This structured approach meant strategic leaders focused on outcomes and implications, operational leaders learned how technology would change their workflows, and technical leaders provided the implementation details. This model enabled effective dialogue without overwhelming anyone. Nestlé's Digital Acceleration Report (2021) documented that the approach significantly improved cross-functional collaboration on AI initiatives and accelerated decision-making around technology investments.

One of the most critical skills now is the ability to ask good questions. Simon Lucas put it well in our research interview: "The most important skill set probably in our industry and plenty of others in the years ahead is going to be framing questions... figuring out a way of asking the right question in order to get the right answer."

Prompting is a useful analogy. AI models like ChatGPT respond differently depending on how you ask. A vague prompt such as:

"Give me a plan to improve our customer experience"

Returns generic suggestions: train staff, gather feedback, and upgrade systems. It's the business equivalent of fluff.

However, a more detailed version of the prompt will produce better results:

"You're a senior CX consultant advising a UK-based retail bank with declining Net Promoter Scores across digital channels. You have access to customer complaints, call centre transcripts, and digital journey analytics. Your task is to create a 3-month action plan to improve the digital customer experience. Focus on quick wins that can be delivered with existing resources. Highlight areas where internal processes are causing delays or confusion. Format the output as: (1) Problem, (2) Recommendation, (3) Expected Outcome."

That prompt produces insight. Specific, usable, actionable advice. The same model, two very different results. The only difference was how the question was framed. The point here is not about prompting skills for their own sake but about how clarity of thought shapes clarity of action.

Moving Forward

The challenges and insights we've explored throughout this chapter aren't theoretical abstractions—they're practical realities already affecting your organisation. The key is to act on them with intentionality before misalignment undermines your AI initiatives.

Our research with successful companies points to five specific actions that create meaningful C-suite alignment:

First, make different perspectives explicit. Schedule structured discussions where functional leaders articulate their AI priorities, concerns, and success criteria. These conversations reveal alignment gaps that would otherwise remain hidden beneath superficial agreement. Consider using a simple framework where each executive answers: "What does AI success look like for my function in one year? What risks concern me most? What dependencies do I see that others might not?"

Second, create shared measurement frameworks. Develop metrics that connect technical performance to business outcomes, ensuring everyone evaluates AI initiatives against consistent standards. When LVMH introduced their "Connected Value Framework" in 2021, they significantly reduced cross-functional friction by ensuring marketing, operations and finance teams all measured success through multiple lenses.

Third, implement tiered knowledge development. Not everyone needs the same level of AI expertise, but everyone needs enough to participate meaningfully in strategic decisions. Structure learning journeys appropriate to different roles rather than attempting to make everyone a technical expert.

Fourth, establish multi-speed governance. Create different approval and implementation paths for different types of AI initiatives based on their risk profile and strategic importance. This approach acknowledges that not all AI applications demand the same level of scrutiny or pace.

Fifth, build an integrated risk assessment. Develop comprehensive risk frameworks that address technical, financial, ethical, and regulatory dimensions of AI initiatives. When executives evaluate risk through multiple lenses, they make more balanced decisions that neither ignore legitimate concerns nor allow a single risk dimension to dominate.

Most importantly, keep the conversation alive. Alignment isn't a task you complete; it's a practice you maintain. As AI evolves, so will your decisions, your structures, and your approaches to risk.

As Christoph Debus told us: "Accept that every process will be impacted by AI and see AI as your friend." That mindset—open, thoughtful, and collaborative—may be the single most powerful advantage a leadership team can cultivate in the age of AI. Those who master this alignment will find themselves able to move with both speed and wisdom, while their competitors remain caught in cycles of enthusiasm followed by caution, never quite harnessing AI's full potential.

Chapter 9
THE FUTURE OF WORK PARADOX

In 2021, global insurance provider AXA faced a critical challenge in its claims processing department. Customer satisfaction was declining as processing times for complex claims stretched to over three weeks. Traditional automation hadn't solved the problem because it couldn't handle the nuanced judgment required for evaluating unique situations.

Rather than simply hiring more claims adjusters or implementing standard automation, AXA took a fundamentally different approach. They created what they termed "augmented teams" – partnerships between experienced adjusters and AI systems designed to work conversationally with their human counterparts. These systems could independently review claim documentation, identify patterns from similar historical cases, and suggest appropriate responses while explaining their reasoning.

The results were remarkable. By early 2023, AXA had reduced complex claim processing times by 68% while improving accuracy rates by 23%. Most significantly, they maintained the same number of claims professionals, but the nature of their work transformed dramatically. Instead of spending hours reviewing documentation, adjusters now focused on edge cases requiring human judgment, customer communication, and teaching the AI systems to handle new claim scenarios.

"We didn't replace our claims teams – we completely reimagined how they work," explained Thomas Buberl, AXA's CEO, in their 2023 Digital Transformation Report. "Our people now spend their time where human intelligence adds the most value, while our AI systems handle routine analysis. It's not about replacement; it's about amplification of human capability."

The workplace is undergoing a profound transformation, and as leaders, we face a critical choice: to rewire our organisations for this new reality or find ourselves increasingly irrelevant. This isn't about incremental change—it's about fundamentally rethinking who does what, how work gets done, and what it means to lead in an era where AI isn't just a tool but a teammate.

Beyond Simple Replacement or Augmentation

The simplistic notion that AI will either replace workers or merely supplement them misses the more complex reality emerging across industries. Organisations leading in AI adoption are discovering a third path: the creation of hybrid or "synthetic" teams where humans and AI systems collaborate through increasingly natural interfaces.

Research published in the MIT Sloan Management Review found that AI adoption creates hybrid roles where "soft skills become primary differentiators" as technical tasks shift to AI systems. This finding was validated by Siemens' Amberg electronics plant transformation, which increased output by 23% while growing roles requiring human judgment rather than technical execution.

Unlike previous waves of automation that primarily affected manual labour, this shift impacts knowledge workers at all levels. The World Economic Forum's 2023 Future of Jobs Report estimates that while 83 million jobs may be displaced by AI, 69 million new roles will emerge specifically focused on human-AI collaboration. The net effect isn't elimination but transformation.

Building Synthetic Teams

We've coined the term "Synthetic Teams" to describe this emerging organisational unit. These teams combine human employees with AI agents, communicating through natural language to achieve shared objectives. This isn't science fiction—it's happening now in forward-thinking organisations.

At Goldman Sachs, financial analysts work alongside AI systems that independently monitor markets, generate reports, and flag anomalies without constant oversight. These AI teammates handle predictable analyses while escalating complex decisions to human counterparts. The banking giant hasn't eliminated analyst positions; they've transformed what analysts do, shifting them toward work that demands uniquely human judgment.

Deloitte provides another compelling example with its AI-enhanced audit teams. As detailed in their 2023 report "Transforming Audit Through AI," their approach pairs human auditors with AI systems that handle data extraction and pattern recognition, while the auditors focus on client relationships and judgment-intensive analyses. The results include 40% faster audit completions and more comprehensive risk identification.

What makes synthetic teams different from earlier human-computer collaboration is the conversational interface.

From Passive Tools to Active Partners

The most transformative development in this domain is the shift from passive AI tools that respond only when prompted to active systems that proactively take action to achieve specified goals. These systems observe, decide, and act independently within defined boundaries.

Gartner's research indicates that by the end of 2025, 25% of enterprises will deploy such proactive AI systems, doubling to 50% by 2027. These aren't future projections—AI is already reshaping how decisions are made and who makes them.

In a study of over a hundred organisations published in the California Management Review, researchers found that when AI was used to support decision-making, outcomes were delivered faster—on average, decision latency dropped by more than half. At the same time, people felt more satisfied with the results. That's not because machines replaced humans but because they changed the balance. AI handled the heavy lifting around data and analysis, freeing people to focus on judgment, context, and ethics.

German manufacturing conglomerate Bosch demonstrates this approach in practice. In their automotive components division, they've deployed specialised AI systems to support teams in making faster, more informed choices. According to their 2023 Industry 4.0 Report, their approach follows a clear pattern: let AI gather and structure the data, but keep humans in charge of the values and trade-offs. It's a "complementary decision" model—not automation for its own sake, but partnership with purpose.

The direction of travel is clear. The World Economic Forum expects nearly half of routine managerial tasks to be supported by AI by 2027. That means it's not just workflows that will need redesigning—it's how we measure performance.

When Anyone Can Create Digital Solutions

The combination of low-code/no-code platforms with generative AI has created what we call the "vibe coding" revolution. Rather than writing technical specifications or code, non-technical professionals now describe what they want to build in conversational language, and AI translates these descriptions into functional software.

This democratisation of design and coding fundamentally alters who gets to build digital solutions. IKEA's recent initiative allowed store managers to modify customer experience features without engineering support. Using natural language descriptions, retail managers created personalised recommendation systems that previously would have required months of development work. As reported in IKEA's 2023 Digital Innovation Review, this approach reduced development time for customer experience improvements by 76%.

The implications extend beyond faster development. When anyone can create software solutions, organisations become more adaptable. Teams don't wait for IT departments—they solve their own problems as they arise.

Curiosity Outweighs Technical Skill

This new technology landscape demands a fundamental mindset shift from "I wish we could" to "What if we tried?" Leaders with strong digital curiosity but no coding background are outperforming technically trained managers who lack this exploratory drive.

McKinsey's research established that digitally curious leaders generate 2.3x more innovation pipelines than peers, a finding operationalised by companies like IBM and Accenture. These organisations now formally assess digital curiosity during hiring and promotion processes. They measure it through scenario-based assessments: "Here's a business problem and access to AI tools—what would you build to solve it?"

The French multinational energy company TotalEnergies provides a compelling example of this approach in practice. Their 2022 initiative, "Digital Explorers", identified and empowered employees with high digital curiosity regardless of their technical background. As documented in their 2023 Sustainability and Climate Report, these employees, when paired with AI tools, generated 147 operational improvements that collectively reduced carbon emissions by 1.8 million tons while improving production efficiency by 11%.

The most valuable employees in this environment aren't those with deep technical skills but those who constantly ask "What if?" and then use AI tools to explore answers. This exploratory mindset represents a form of literacy as essential as reading and writing were in previous eras.

When Middle Management Faces Disruption

Traditional management hierarchies face unprecedented pressure when junior team members can build sophisticated solutions through AI collaboration. What happens to managers who lack both technical understanding and digital curiosity?

One executive, an experienced NED and ex-CFO we spoke with, observed this resistance at the board level: "I've seen very little leadership on AI. In fact, to me, it always feels like I've been the one who has been trying to push and drive the conversation, and I got very, very little back." This disconnect between leadership levels threatens organisational effectiveness in the AI era.

Research from MIT Sloan Management Review found that middle managers without AI literacy faced a 37% higher role elimination rate than their AI-fluent peers. The issue wasn't technical skill per se but the inability to effectively evaluate and direct the work of these new human-AI teams.

One CEO we spoke to put it bluntly: "Past success can be your biggest liability in the AI era...I look at my experienced analysts today and think, who knows…in a few years, perhaps even faster, I don't need the analysts anymore." This recognition—that previous organisational structures may become liabilities—should prompt serious reflection among leaders at all levels.

Rethinking Talent in the AI Era

The rise of synthetic teams demands a complete reimagining of talent management. When everyone has access to powerful AI teammates, what differentiates high performers becomes how effectively they leverage these digital partners.

Unilever's talent strategy overhaul explicitly recognised this reality. According to their 2023 Future of Work report, their job descriptions now specify human skills and expectations for AI collaboration. Performance reviews include metrics on effective synthetic team management. Compensation packages reflect the amplified impact employees can achieve when effectively partnering with AI.

The retention challenge grows even more acute when entrepreneurship becomes drastically more accessible through AI. Y Combinator reported a 43% increase in solo founders using AI as core team members in 2023. One founder described their operation as "me, Claude, and GitHub Copilot—that's the entire company."

How will you keep talent in your organisation when they can spin up a startup over a weekend, using AI to handle tasks that previously required entire teams?

Rapid Prototyping Becomes Essential

The "vibe coding" revolution paired with proactive AI dramatically compresses development timelines. What once took months now takes days or hours. This acceleration favours a specific approach: relentless experimentation through minimal viable products (MVPS).

Christoph Debus described this shift through his company's "Flix Labs" initiative: "We have 600 people who just do coding. They are given three days and are completely free to try anything. It was mind-blowing. They came up with such a tremendous amount of creativity." This compressed innovation cycle represents the new normal.

Organisations thriving in this environment build quick prototypes, gather immediate feedback, and iterate rapidly. The cost of failure plummets when AI can generate new solutions in hours rather than months. When telecommunications provider Vodafone shifted to AI-augmented development in 2023, they reduced customer experience improvement cycles from quarters to weeks, according to their Digital Transformation Annual Report.

Siemens Mini Case Study

In 2022, Siemens began a comprehensive transformation of their Amberg electronics plant, creating one of the most advanced examples of synthetic teamwork in manufacturing. Their approach offers valuable lessons for leaders in any industry.

Digital Teammates on the Production Line

Siemens didn't frame their initiative as automation but as augmentation. They developed Digital Twin systems that worked alongside human operators, handling repetitive monitoring tasks while escalating anomalies to their human counterparts.

What made their approach distinctive was the natural language interface. Operators communicated with the system conversationally rather than through complex technical interfaces. The AI answered questions like "How's line three performing?" or "Show me yesterday's quality issues" with relevant data visualisations and recommendations.

By 2024, the Amberg plant had increased output by 23% while maintaining the exact workforce headcount. The composition of that workforce, however, changed dramatically, according to Siemens' Digital Enterprise Transformation Report.

Transforming the Existing Workforce

Rather than hiring AI specialists, Siemens invested in transforming their existing workforce. They created a tiered training program that offered employees multiple paths forward.

The program began with fundamental AI literacy—understanding how to communicate effectively with AI systems and interpret their outputs. This training was mandatory for all employees, creating a common language around synthetic teamwork.

Beyond this foundation, employees could choose different specialisation paths. Some became "AI Orchestrators" who managed multiple AI systems. Others became "Domain Experts" who taught AI systems the nuances of specific manufacturing processes.

This approach aligns with Geeta Malhotra's observation from our interviews: "Domain expertise becomes all the more important because we are talking of far more robust prediction... The niche will become all the more valuable." Specialisation doesn't disappear in the AI era—it transforms.

Siemens avoided creating an elite class of AI experts separate from factory operations. They integrated AI capabilities across all roles, ensuring that every team included both human and digital teammates working in concert.

Leading Through the Transition

Perhaps most instructive was Siemens's approach to change management. They recognised that synthetic teams create profound anxiety when poorly introduced.

Their leadership team began by openly addressing the workforce's concerns. They presented specific examples of how jobs would change rather than making vague promises about "new opportunities." They created shadowing programs where employees could observe synthetic teams in action before joining them.

Despite initial anxiety, the result was remarkable: worker satisfaction scores increased by 22% after implementation. Employees reported feeling their work had become more meaningful as routine tasks shifted to digital teammates.

Christoph Debus also noted the importance of working with employee representatives: "A good union and a good works council... they are usually smart people. They understand the business processes often better than management... The only thing they require is to deal fairly with the impacted people." This focus on fairness and transparency proves essential when introducing synthetic teams.

Moving Forward

As we've explored throughout this chapter, the future of work isn't humans versus machines but humans with machines—working together in ways that leverage each other's unique strengths. This partnership creates challenges but also unprecedented opportunities for those prepared to embrace it.

Based on our research with leading organisations, we recommend five specific actions to prepare your organisation for the synthetic team era:

- ***Redefine roles around human strengths.*** Identify where human judgment, creativity, and emotional intelligence add the most value, and redesign roles to emphasise these elements while shifting routine analytical tasks to AI. Unilever's job taxonomy project provides an excellent template for this approach.

- ***Build digital curiosity, not just technical skills.*** Create assessment frameworks that identify and reward digital curiosity across all levels of your organisation. TotalEnergies' Digital Explorers program offers a practical model for identifying and empowering the digitally curious.

- ***Establish ethical guidelines for AI teammates.*** Develop clear principles governing when AI systems can act independently and when they must escalate decisions to human team members. AXA's "Human-AI Collaboration Framework" provides a useful starting point.

- ***Invest in conversational interfaces.*** The effectiveness of synthetic teams depends heavily on natural communication between human and AI teammates. Prioritise systems that minimise technical barriers to this collaboration.

- ***Create rapid experimentation cultures.*** Establish dedicated time, resources, and recognition for teams to build quick prototypes with AI tools. The compressed development timelines enabled by AI make experimentation less costly and more valuable than ever before.

The organisations thriving in this new era share common characteristics: they view AI as teammates rather than tools, they cultivate digital curiosity across all levels, they embrace rapid experimentation, and they reimagine management for synthetic team effectiveness.

Simon Lucas captured the essence of this transition in our interview: "It's about becoming an organisation that places far more emphasis on interpersonal skills, communication skills, relationship-building skills and probably less emphasis on attention to detail and process rigour." The human elements of leadership become more valuable, not less, as AI handles increasingly complex technical tasks.

Most importantly, successful organisations recognise that the window for adaptation is narrowing. The pace of change continues to accelerate.

The essential question isn't whether your organisation will incorporate synthetic teams—that's inevitable. The question is whether you'll lead this transformation or be forced to follow competitors who move more quickly. Will you be among those who rewire their approach to this new reality, or will you find yourself struggling to catch up as the landscape transforms around you?

Chapter 10
THE CULTURAL CONTRADICTION

In 2021, Rolls-Royce grappled with a significant challenge at its Derby aerospace facility. Despite substantial investments in advanced technologies, their digital transformation efforts were faltering. The tools functioned flawlessly in controlled settings but struggled to gain acceptance on the factory floor.

"We had world-class tools and talented engineers, but we weren't seeing the results we expected," noted then-CEO Warren East in the 2022 Annual Report. The core issue wasn't technological—it was cultural. Deep-rooted hierarchies and established processes, which had long ensured engineering precision, were inadvertently hindering innovation. Engineers were hesitant to trust computer-generated insights over their experience, and managers feared disrupting proven workflows.

To address this, Rolls-Royce introduced cross-functional "Digital

Pioneer" teams, blending seasoned engineers with digital specialists. These teams were empowered to challenge existing processes and experiment in controlled environments, with success measured by learning outcomes rather than immediate productivity. Although by 2022, digital adoption had risen by 64%, and production efficiency improved by 18% in augmented processes, the business's overall performance had not. There seemed to be a disconnect between digital willingness and operational outcomes.

Fast forward to 2023, Tufan Erginbilgiç assumed the role of CEO, confronting what he described as a "burning platform" of a business that was still underperforming. Under his leadership, Rolls-Royce embarked on a comprehensive transformation, emphasising cultural change alongside strategic realignment. The results have been remarkable. By early 2025, the company's share price had soared from approximately 91p in late 2022 to over 730p, marking a significant turnaround. Operating profits increased by 57% to £2.5 billion, and the company reinstated its dividend after a five-year hiatus.

Erginbilgiç's approach focused on mobilising the workforce with a clear purpose and alignment. He emphasised that transformation isn't merely about restructuring but about instilling a performance-driven culture. This cultural shift has been pivotal in accelerating digital and AI adoption across the organisation.

Rolls-Royce's journey underscores a critical insight: technological advancements alone aren't sufficient. It's the cultural context—the willingness to embrace change, challenge norms, and foster collaboration—alongside inspiring leadership that determines the success of digital transformation initiatives.

Organisations can talk a good game on AI and digital transformation. They invest in tools, experiment with pilots, and hire the talent. But when you look more closely, many of these efforts stall—not because the technology isn't ready, but because the organisation isn't. Culture, not capability, remains the most significant barrier. The most promising strategies often falter not in the design phase but in the day-to-day interactions, governance patterns, and behavioural defaults that reveal how an organisation really works.

This chapter explores the human side of transformation—how culture either enables or stifles change. It's about the gaps between stated ambition and lived reality. We look at three specific cultural tensions: the clash between legacy thinking and digital mindsets, the challenge of attracting and retaining talent in a world where digital fluency is a differentiator, and the paradox of wanting innovation without disrupting stability.

Throughout, we ask one central question: Is your culture built for what AI-driven digital transformation needs, or built to resist it?

The Adoption Fault Line

There is a temptation to think of new technologies as something you can bolt on—new tools layered onto familiar structures, or like a layer of digital paint to freshen up what lies beneath it. But that's rarely how it works. When advanced technologies are introduced into organisations that are still shaped by rigid hierarchies and cautious, rules-based cultures, something starts to push back. And it's not the tech. It often exposes what we call an 'adoption fault line'.

MIT Sloan's 2023 research puts this plainly. Eighty-five per cent of IT leaders said that cultural resistance, not technical barriers, was the main reason digital initiatives underperformed. The markers of resistance are familiar: data held in silos, experimentation viewed as risky rather than necessary, and decisions filtered through the lens of how things have always been done.

Keith Grimes, the founder of Curistica, a clinical product innovation consultancy, puts it sharply: "The least interesting thing about digitalisation is when you digitise the status quo." That tendency—to treat new technology as a faster version of the existing system—runs deep. It's not always deliberate. Sometimes, people simply can't see what's possible, only what feels familiar.

Have you noticed this pattern in your own organisation? Projects that start with excitement but gradually conform to established ways of working? Pilots that show promise but never scale beyond their initial scope?

The cultural shift required for real adoption is not about enthusiasm. It's about behaviour. Organisations that succeed behave differently. They test ideas quickly and visibly. They build structures that allow junior voices to challenge senior assumptions. They create space for failure that doesn't threaten careers. And they reward those who stretch the model, not just those who manage it.

BMW's cultural evolution is a case in point. Shifting from an engineering-led hierarchy to a digitally enabled innovation model wasn't cosmetic—it meant giving junior engineers the licence to question assumptions, including those of their more senior colleagues. The result wasn't just faster prototyping (40% improvement, according to BMW's 2024 report)—it was higher engagement, particularly among younger, technically fluent staff.

This kind of change demands more than a handful of training programmes or awareness campaigns. It demands leadership behaviours that signal new norms. It means clarifying that curiosity is expected, disagreement is safe, and digital transformation isn't a side project for specialists—it's everyone's business.

Lieutenant-General Sir Tom Copinger-Symes, the Deputy Commander of the UK Strategic Command, explains, "I still run across all sorts of things in meetings that have to have very serious decisions at the end.... and the leaders are decisive then. But sometimes you need a conversation where the decision isn't at the end of the conversation, where you're exploring things you don't know about. Even if you could get people at the top, you go out of your way to bring people from the organisation so that they can see the board and the board can see them, and you can have an extraordinary conversation."

It also requires reframing the role of failure. In many legacy cultures, failure is something to be hidden or explained away. In digital initiatives, especially those involving new models or untested use cases, failure at some stage is inevitable. The challenge is how failure is interpreted. Is it seen as incompetence, or as a sign that the team is genuinely exploring?

This is where leadership tone matters. Leaders who frame early setbacks as part of the process, rather than indicators of poor performance, create the psychological safety required for genuine experimentation. Without that experimentation, digital initiatives rarely move past the prototype stage.

Winning the Talent Race

Culture shows up most visibly in who wants to work for you and who doesn't. The new generation of talent isn't just looking for a salary and a title. Increasingly, they're asking a more pointed question: Will I get the opportunity to work with advanced technologies and learn how to use them well?

PwC's 2023 survey found that nearly three-quarters of Gen Z professionals actively avoid roles that lack clear digital upskilling opportunities. It's a striking statistic that should worry any organisation that is still treating digital fluency as a niche skill for IT teams.

For a growing number of candidates, working with modern technology isn't just a bonus. It's a sign that a company is thinking ahead. And they're not wrong. In most industries, fluency with digital tools is quickly becoming as essential as knowing how to run a meeting or write a report.

When was the last time you reviewed your talent proposition through this lens? Do your job descriptions highlight opportunities to learn and apply digital skills? Does your interview process explore candidates' curiosity about emerging technologies?

The most forward-looking employers have started to adjust their pitch. It's no longer just, "We'll pay you well and promote you." It's, "We'll help you learn how to lead in a digital world." That message, when backed by real learning programmes, has impact.

Siemens provides a good example. Their tiered training model offers baseline digital literacy to all staff while giving those in more complex or technical roles a clear path to developing deeper expertise. It's not presented as optional. It's seen as part of professional growth—something you do not because you're falling behind but because you're building forward.

At HSBC, digital literacy became part of the company's visible culture. Team members who completed certain milestones were given digital badges, which were integrated into email signatures and org charts. These weren't gimmicks. They signalled commitment, capability, and confidence. According to their 2023 Annual Report, retention among key managers rose by 27% following the programme's implementation.

But talent retention isn't just about learning. It's about how that learning is recognised and used. In too many companies, staff complete digital training only to return to roles that don't offer opportunities to apply those skills. That mismatch between investment and usage erodes trust quickly.

To avoid this, organisations must map learning to real opportunities. That means creating projects, secondments, and shadowing opportunities where newly acquired digital skills can be applied. It also means updating performance reviews and promotion criteria to reflect technological collaboration, not just delivery against traditional KPIs.

And then there is the human dimension. As Paul Dongha, Natwest Bank's head of Ethics and Strategy, said, "Driving transformation doesn't happen in the abstract. People lead it, and ideally, those are people who have built trust and credibility in the organisation."

Each organisation has its informal influencers—the people others watch before deciding how seriously to take something. If those people are excited by AI, others follow. If they are sceptical, it can stall adoption across entire functions. The challenge is identifying these figures early and engaging them directly, not through persuasion but through involvement.

The Innovation-Stability Paradox

One of the toughest tensions in AI adoption is that you're being asked to experiment with something new inside a system that has been optimised for consistency. Innovation and stability are not natural partners. And yet, both are essential.

Executives often ask how they can encourage bold AI thinking without compromising service delivery or increasing risk. There's no magic answer. However, a pattern exists: successful organisations build in structural room for both.

Gartner's "70/20/10" model offers a helpful framework. Seventy per cent of AI work focuses on core processes—places where automation can improve efficiency and consistency. Twenty per cent goes to adjacent opportunities, often specific to business units. Ten per cent is allocated to high-risk, high-reward exploration. That balance is important. Too much innovation without discipline is chaotic, and too much discipline without innovation is stagnant.

Governance is what makes the difference. Organisations that succeed here often run dual-track models. One track governs customer-facing AI tightly, with formal sign-offs and risk reviews. The other track allows for experimentation—sandbox environments where failure is part of the process, not a career threat. Deloitte's research suggests companies using this approach see more than twice the return on AI investment.

Paul Dongha explained that his team secured credibility by aligning AI projects with established enterprise risk frameworks. "We're doing work that's leveraging our enterprise risk management framework for their [AI] work. And we are treated as first-class citizens in the boardroom... So at that point, there isn't pushback." Governance done well doesn't slow things down. It gives innovation permission to exist.

But governance alone isn't the solution. The broader cultural pattern matters. As Mikko Tepponen, The COO of Mining giant FDSmidth puts it, "...it starts with corporate agility and agile ways of working... because the pace of changes has become so fast, you cannot rely on the old way of working... for me, there must be more of a fundamental cultural change that needs to be put into place." Hierarchy slows down agility. Silos limit collaboration. The more you can shift from control to coordination, the faster AI ideas can move.

Tepponen further emphasises the structural dimensions: "...the more hierarchical and more centred you are around your silos, the harder it becomes; the more you actually work in a full agile mode or where structures of the company are not that important... if you can design an organisational structure that is not about the hierarchy and more about how do you actually collaborate and work, I think that's for me the key."

Teams experimenting with new models must also be given the psychological licence to fail. If experimental initiatives are judged by the same criteria as core operations, they will be killed off too early. Boards and senior executives need to understand the difference between delivery KPIs and exploration KPIs. The former measures output, while the latter measures learning.

A Cultural Transformation Model

Given these cultural contradictions, how should leaders approach transformation? While many organisations adopt piecemeal approaches, successful AI integration requires deliberate cultural evolution guided by clear methodology.

Our research points to a four-phase transformation model adapted from Perceptyx (2025).

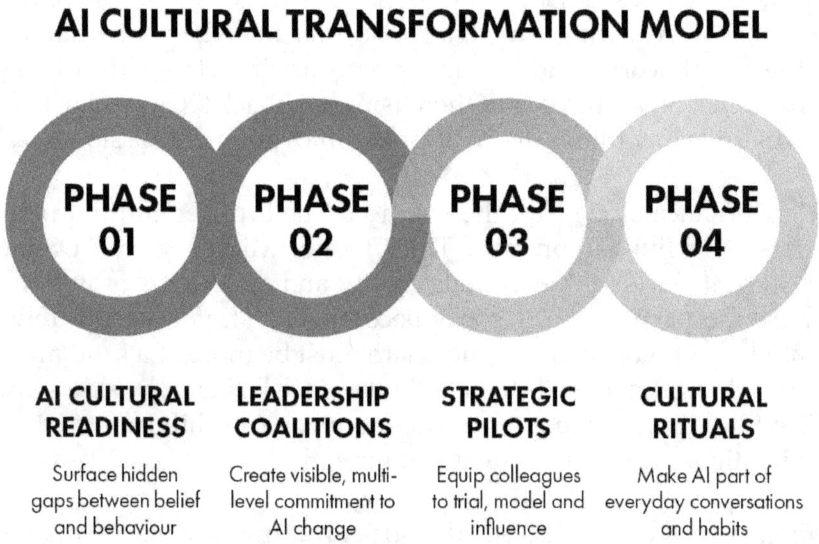

The first phase involves the honest diagnosis of cultural AI readiness. Leading organisations conduct thorough cultural audits specifically focused on AI readiness. Microsoft's approach examines twelve dimensions spanning leadership alignment, risk tolerance, collaboration patterns, and technical capability. This diagnostic depth prevents the common trap of surface-level assessments that miss deeper contradictions.

However, meaningful diagnosis extends beyond formal assessments to ground-level reality. One of our interviewees highlighted this gap between perception and practice: "Sometimes we found that the details of the assessments, where we had asked people to rank what they needed versus where they believed we actually were, were very marked". Her candid observation reminds us that cultural self-perception often differs dramatically from actual practices, particularly regarding digital sophistication.

The second phase requires building leadership coalitions. BMW's approach was to institute "AI Translator" workshops specifically designed for executive teams. These sessions went beyond technical demonstrations to address fundamental questions of decision authority, risk tolerance, and cultural implications.

This alignment cannot remain confined to executive suites. Graham Donoghue, the CEO of Forge Holidays, articulates this challenge vividly: "The most difficult thing was that, at times, it felt as if it was just me... alone, standing at the top of the mountain, telling people what to do. It wasn't enough. I needed people to be doing it in action, and I needed them to be recruiting other AI guardians and creating this sort of a flow through the organisation."

His mountaineering metaphor captures an essential truth—transformation demands visible champions at multiple organisational levels. A lone but enthusiastic executive, no matter how genuine, will prove insufficient unless others in the organisation take up the leadership role on AI.

The third phase focuses on strategic pilots with embedded champions. Siemens exemplifies this approach with its factory floor "AI ambassadors"—respected operators who receive additional training and explicit permission to experiment with AI applications in their daily work. These embedded champions simultaneously demonstrate AI's practical value while modelling new cultural norms.

The final phase establishes enterprise-wide cultural rituals. Vodafone institutionalised monthly "AI Demo Days" where cross-functional teams showcase applications regardless of completion status. These events normalise experimentation, celebrate learning from failure, and reinforce collaboration across traditional boundaries.

The urgency of thoughtful yet deliberate cultural transformation cannot be overstated. Perceptyx's research (2025) reveals that 37% of employees report worsened job satisfaction in haphazard AI implementations.

This striking figure underscores that cultural transformation isn't merely about adoption speed but fundamentally concerns employee experience.

Leadership's Cultural Leverage Points

Ultimately, cultural transformation depends on leadership behaviours that model new expectations while addressing legitimate concerns. Our research identifies three non-technical capabilities that distinguish effective AI-era leaders.

Trust Architects

First, successful leaders serve as trust architects who establish transparent decision rights regarding AI applications. They clearly articulate where AI provides recommendations versus autonomous decisions and which domains remain exclusively human. For instance, many organisations implement explicit policies stating: "Humans always finalise hiring and promotion decisions." These boundaries create psychological safety that accelerates adoption.

Simon Lucas articulates how this trust-building connects to broader cultural evolution: "The cultural transformation lies behind that is... about becoming an organisation that places far more emphasis on the interpersonal skills, the communication skills, the relationship building skill and probably less emphasis on the attention to detail and the process rigour."

He further notes: "That is a big shift because I think the sort of people who we've tended to hire in the past have been very diligent, detail-minded people... And probably what we'll need more of in the future is more of an extroverted outward focus." His observation highlights that AI's automation of routine analytical tasks requires leaders who excel at relationship-building and complex communication skills that build trust during transformation.

Anxiety Doctors

Second, effective leaders function as 'anxiety doctors' who directly address implementation anxieties. Microsoft's research into AI's impact on productivity revealed that tools like Copilot significantly reduce the mental effort required for routine tasks. In studies, users reported a 58% decrease in task-related fatigue when using AI assistance. Moreover, 72% agreed that AI helped them spend less mental effort on mundane tasks.

This capability involves acknowledging legitimate concerns while redirecting energy toward constructive learning. Rather than dismissing and labelling fears as a form of resistance, skilled leaders recognise anxiety as natural and provide structured outlets for addressing it.

Storytellers

Third, transformative leaders act as storytellers-in-chief who craft compelling stories that reframe AI as augmentation rather than replacement. Salesforce exemplifies this approach with its "AI as Colleague" concept, which explicitly positions AI tools as team members with complementary capabilities rather than job substitutes. This reframing reduced turnover by 18% (Salesforce, 2023).

Lieutenant-General Sir Tom Copinger-Symes advocated the power of storytelling in the digital transformation that the British Army embarked on in 2020. "Data convinces the mind, but stories move the culture. If you don't shape the story, someone else will—and it may not help. Leadership isn't just about setting direction; it's about owning the narrative that makes change matter."

Moving Forward

Cultural change rarely announces itself. It shows up in tone, tempo, and trust. If your AI efforts feel slow, stalled or politically sensitive, it may be a sign that the culture underneath isn't aligned.

And while culture can feel nebulous, its impact is very real. It affects who joins your company. It shapes who stays. It determines which ideas survive first contact with reality. And it defines what kind of future your organisation will be capable of building.

Based on our research with organisations successfully coping with this cultural shift, we recommend five specific actions:

- ***Start with an honest cultural assessment.*** Conduct a thorough assessment of your organisation's AI readiness, examining not just technical capability but psychological safety, risk tolerance, and decision-making patterns. Microsoft's twelve-dimensional assessment provides a useful template.

- ***Build multi-level champions.*** Identify and empower respected individuals at every organisational level to serve as AI champions. Siemens' "AI ambassadors" program demonstrates how embedding champions within operational teams accelerates adoption.

- ***Create dual governance tracks.*** Establish separate governance approaches for core AI applications versus experimental initiatives. Deloitte's research shows this dual-track approach delivers twice the return on AI investment.

- ***Redesign talent processes.*** Update recruitment, development, and promotion criteria to reflect AI literacy requirements. HSBC's digital badge program provides a model for making AI capabilities visible and valued.

- ***Institute cultural rituals.*** Create regular events and practices that normalise AI experimentation. Vodafone's monthly "AI Demo Days" show how structured rituals can reshape cultural expectations.

The contradiction at the heart of many AI programmes is that leaders say they want transformation, but unconsciously reward the behaviours that maintain the status quo. That's not about bad faith. It's about default habits—what's comfortable, familiar, and safe.

Transformation doesn't start with a new tool or a new hire. It starts with being honest about what your culture really enables—and what it quietly resists. Only then can the shift begin. And that is a leadership task. And the first question you, as leaders, need to ask yourselves should be: "Is our culture built for what AI needs—or built to resist it?

Chapter 11
THE CAREER CROSSROADS

In 2022, Alan Jope, then-CEO of Unilever, faced a pivotal moment. After nearly four decades with the consumer goods giant, he was contemplating his final leadership chapter before retirement. The company was investing heavily in digital transformation and AI, and Jope had to decide how deeply to involve himself in this technological shift.

"I realised I was at a crossroads," Jope explained during a 2023 Financial Times interview. "I could either commit to becoming genuinely fluent in these new technologies, which would require significant personal investment, or I could focus on ensuring we had the right talent and culture to support this transformation while I concentrated on areas where my experience added the most value."

Jope chose the latter path. Rather than attempting to become Unilever's AI champion, he recruited a chief digital and technology officer with deep expertise and focused his own efforts on mentoring the next generation of leaders and reinforcing the company's purpose-driven culture during technological change. This choice wasn't a retreat—it was a strategic decision about where his leadership could best serve the organisation in its final phase.

This moment now plays out in organisations everywhere. What's changed isn't just the technology; it's what leadership is starting to mean.

For years, we've talked about "people leaders" and "technology leaders" as if they were two distinct camps. That separation is collapsing. Executives today face a very real choice—whether to step forward into a more AI-literate leadership role or to focus intentionally on the human side of leadership, where long-standing experience and judgement remain vital. This isn't about picking sides. It's about being honest with yourself about where your strengths lie and where you want to focus. Sitting on the fence no longer works.

The Vulnerability of Indecision

Many try to take a middle route. They acknowledge AI matters but leave the details to others. It feels pragmatic, but it's becoming less and less viable. Organisations need leaders who are either prepared to build real digital capability or who are ready to double down on the human skills that AI can't replicate. Sitting quietly in the middle is the most vulnerable position of all.

One of our interviewees, an FTSE-100 CFO with years of experience, shared: "I attend the AI meetings, but I'm not sure what I'm adding. I find myself nodding at the technical parts while wondering whether I should get more involved, or step back entirely." It's a familiar story. And it's not a lack of intelligence, it's a lack of clarity. This kind of drift creates a career limbo. You're not building a new capability. But you're not owning your current one, either.

Have you found yourself in meetings about AI or digital transformation where you're present but not truly engaged? Are you making contributions that genuinely shape the direction, or simply approving others' recommendations?

In a 2023 Harvard Business Review survey of 500 C-suite executives, 67% reported feeling "partially engaged but not fully confident" in technology discussions. This middle ground is increasingly risky as boards and shareholders expect clear leadership positioning on digital transformation.

If you've taken the dQ assessment earlier in the book, you'll already have a sense of where you stand—across everything from data strategy to AI literacy, from human-AI collaboration to security and ethics. That's your map. But the key is deciding where to go from here, because in this new era of leadership, there are really only two coherent paths forward.

Two Paths, Both Valuable

Both paths are valid. One leans into change, building new capabilities to lead through AI. The other anchors leadership within the human skills that organisations must retain as technology advances. What matters most is that you choose—actively, deliberately, and in full view.

Luis Gallego, CEO of International Airlines Group (IAG), exemplifies the first path. Despite being well into his career, Gallego committed to extensive AI education, including completing MIT's "AI in Business Strategy" program in 2022. "I decided I couldn't delegate understanding these technologies if I wanted to lead our transformation," he explained in a 2023 interview with El País. "It wasn't about becoming a technical expert, but about being fluent enough to make strategic decisions."

His investment has paid dividends. IAG has implemented AI across customer service, maintenance, and route optimisation. Gallego's hands-on involvement has accelerated adoption while ensuring these initiatives align with broader business objectives. IAG's post-pandemic recovery has outpaced many competitors, with their 2023 Annual Report attributing €380 million in operational savings to AI-driven efficiencies.

Conversely, Emma Walmsley, CEO of GSK, demonstrates the equally valuable second path. Rather than positioning herself as GSK's AI champion, Walmsley ensures the pharmaceutical giant maintains its human expertise and ethical standards while embracing AI for drug discovery. In GSK's 2023 Annual Report, she emphasises: "My role isn't to be our AI expert—we have brilliant people for that. My responsibility is ensuring we apply these powerful tools in service of our purpose and values, protecting what makes GSK special while embracing what makes us more effective."

This approach has served GSK well—their AI-enhanced drug discovery platform has accelerated clinical trials while maintaining the company's reputation for scientific rigour and ethical standards.

The REWIRE Framework

If you choose to REWIRE, you're not just trying to 'keep up'—you're preparing to lead from the front. This is about developing the mindset, fluency and confidence to shape AI-driven transformation rather than simply adapting to it. It's not a light touch. However, for those who commit, it opens new leadership possibilities and a longer professional runway.

- ***R – Reality Check:*** Start with honesty. Where are you now—really? This means confronting gaps in your digital literacy, understanding your own resistance points, and recognising where others may already be ahead. It also means looking at your organisation's readiness. Are you surrounded by people who will support your development, or will you need to build new networks? This kind of clarity isn't always comfortable, but it's essential.

- ***E – Engage***: Understanding theory isn't enough. You need to use the tools. Pick one or two AI platforms and start experimenting—not as an expert, but as a learner. Build a habit of engaging daily, even if it's small. Join a short course, shadow a team using AI in their workflow, or set yourself a simple weekly challenge. Once you stop delegating and start engaging, your confidence grows fast.

- ***W – Widen:*** Break out of your usual information loop. Follow digital pioneers in adjacent sectors. Subscribe to sources you wouldn't normally read. Talk to start-ups. Attend events where you're the least technical person in the room. Broadening your context doesn't just expand your vision—it helps you spot possibilities others in your sector may miss.

- ***I – Integrate:*** It's one thing to understand how AI works. It's another to understand how to lead teams that include it. This phase is about learning how to build effective human-AI collaboration, which includes new metrics, new expectations, and, sometimes, new models of decision-making. It also means helping others navigate discomfort. Leading hybrid teams will be one of the core executive capabilities of the next decade.

- ***R – Reshape:*** This is the strategy piece. AI won't just change how you work. It will reshape what your business does, how it competes, and what it looks like operationally. As a leader, you'll need to rethink business models, revisit your assumptions about value, and develop a roadmap that links AI capability with strategic ambition.

- ***E – Evaluate:*** There is no endpoint. This final phase is about setting up regular feedback mechanisms—personal and organisational. What's working? Where are you falling behind? Where has your thinking moved on? Regular review keeps your learning active and stops the common trap of building a plan you forget to revisit.

Marco Wirén, who has championed AI transformation across multiple leadership roles, emphasises this continuous nature of learning: "AI isn't something you simply tick off a checklist. It's much like learning a language – you need to practice regularly and watch your fluency grow over time." This language metaphor is particularly apt—fluency doesn't arrive overnight, nor does it stay without practice. The most effective leaders establish regular rhythms of learning, reflection and practical application rather than treating AI understanding as a one-time achievement.

Equally important is maintaining genuine enthusiasm throughout this journey. As Wirén advises: "Embrace AI with genuine excitement about its possibilities. When leaders show real enthusiasm rather than just going through the motions, everything changes." This mindset matters enormously. When leaders approach AI with curiosity rather than obligation, their learning deepens and their teams notice. The contagious nature of a leader's enthusiasm—or lack thereof—shouldn't be underestimated. Those who genuinely see possibility rather than simply necessity tend to make faster progress and inspire broader adoption across their organisations.

This is a serious commitment. But it comes with rewards: extended relevance, increased impact, and the ability to lead transformation on your terms—not from behind.

Jean-Pascal Tricoire, Executive Chairman of Schneider Electric, followed this path when he realised digital transformation would fundamentally reshape the energy management sector. "I decided I needed to understand these technologies well enough to lead from the front," he explained in a 2022 McKinsey interview. Tricoire dedicated 10 hours weekly to learning technical concepts, working directly with the company's digital team, and visiting customers using advanced technologies.

His commitment transformed not just his leadership but Schneider itself. Between 2018 and 2023, the company evolved from equipment provider to digital solutions leader, with software and digital services growing from 12% to 25% of revenue. Tricoire's personal transformation enabled this corporate evolution.

The RETIRE Framework

Choosing the RETIRE path isn't about stepping back from leadership. It's about stepping into a different kind of leadership—one grounded in perspective, judgment, and the uniquely human qualities that remain essential in times of change.

This is not a retreat, it's a repositioning. And for some, it's the most strategic and satisfying move they can make.

- ***R – Refocus:*** Start by identifying where your real value lies. What do you bring that algorithms can't? That might include institutional memory, deep sector expertise, or the kind of judgment that only comes from experience. Reframing your role in terms of what technology can't replicate is a powerful way to remain central to your organisation's next chapter.

- ***E – Empower:*** You've built up knowledge over the years. Now, it's about sharing it. That could mean mentoring up-and-coming leaders, setting up reverse mentoring arrangements, or shaping formal succession plans. Structured knowledge transfer helps ensure continuity while building trust across generations of leaders.

- ***T – Translate:*** AI can move fast, but values don't. One of the most important roles human-centred leaders can play is helping ensure that, as technology is adopted, organisational principles aren't lost. You become the voice that links emerging capability with enduring culture. You help the business hold on to its identity while still evolving.

- ***I – Influence:*** You may no longer want to—or need to—hold the reins directly. But that doesn't mean stepping away. Influence matters. Whether through formal board positions or informal coaching roles, your ability to shape decisions without controlling them becomes a key contribution. This is about shifting from doing to guiding.

- ***R – Reinforce:*** When disruption happens, people look for steadiness. Human connection, team trust, cultural rituals. These things don't get less important as AI expands; if anything, they become more vital. By reinforcing these bonds, you ensure that technology enhances rather than erodes what makes an organisation worth belonging to.

- ***E – Enable:*** Legacy doesn't mean looking back. It means building something that lasts. That includes thoughtful succession, documented insight, and perhaps an advisory role that allows you to keep contributing on your terms. Your goal isn't just to leave well—it's to leave behind something that works.

Neither path is a fallback. Both are necessary. The only risk lies in refusing to choose.

Rose Marcario, former CEO of Patagonia, exemplifies this approach. After leading the outdoor clothing company through significant growth, she chose to focus on the company's values and environmental mission rather than becoming its digital transformation leader. In her 2021 Stanford Business School guest lecture, she explained: "I recognised my greatest contribution would be reinforcing our purpose and developing leaders who could take the company forward with new technical skills while maintaining our core values."

This focus on what she calls "values-first leadership" enabled Patagonia to embrace digital innovation while strengthening its commitment to environmental activism—a balance that has driven both growth and impact.

Have you considered which aspects of leadership give you the most energy and where your experience could provide the most distinctive value as technology reshapes your organisation?

Understanding Your Decision Factors

So, how do you decide? There's no shortcut, but there are five areas that deserve your attention. These are not personality tests or style preferences—they're real, practical factors that shape your ability to succeed on either path.

Time Horizon

This one's simple but often ignored. If you've got another ten or more years in leadership, then investing deeply in digital capability makes sense—it has time to pay off. But if you're planning to step back within five years, your focus might be better placed on knowledge transfer, culture, and people. That's not about giving up. It's about being realistic. Angela, a COO in her late fifties, put it well: "I realised that trying to become a technical expert in five years didn't make sense. But helping our next-generation leaders grow while keeping the business grounded—that felt like a legacy worth leaving."

Learning Agility

This is less about what you know now and more about how quickly and willingly you learn. Look back. When new technologies emerged in your industry, did you lean in or look for someone else to handle it? Do you get energy from learning new tools, or does it frustrate you?

Motivation

What energises you? Be honest. Some leaders thrive on reinvention while others thrive on consistency. Neither is better. But if you pick a path that doesn't match what gives you energy, you'll burn out. Sandra, a CHRO, told us: "What I love most is seeing people grow. I didn't want to become an AI strategist. But I absolutely want to help our people work well with AI."

Organisational Context

You don't operate in a vacuum. What does your organisation need right now? Are there already strong digital leaders in place? Or does the business lack someone who can provide cultural continuity, ethical oversight, or people-centred thinking?

Legacy

What do you want to be remembered for? Is it your role to lead a breakthrough? Or your role in keeping the business human during change? Both are valid. But they're different. Be clear about the legacy you want to leave. Neil, a European CEO who has just stepped down from running a large division, said it plainly: "I won't be the one to master this new tech. But I can be the one who made sure we used it wisely."

All of these decision factors work best when approached with humility, not ambition. There's no single 'right' path, but there is a right path for you.

The Boston Consulting Group's 2023 report "Leadership Transitions in the AI Era" found that executives who made explicit choices about their role in digital transformation were 3.2 times more likely to report career satisfaction than those who maintained ambiguous positions. This clarity benefits not just individual leaders but their organisations as well.

Making Your Decision

The most effective approach combines structured self-assessment with an external perspective. Complete an honest self-inventory using the questions above. Then, seek feedback from trusted colleagues about where they see your greatest potential contribution. This external perspective often reveals blind spots in your self-assessment.

Consider conducting a "pilot test" by engaging in activities from both paths to assess your energy and effectiveness. Establish clear metrics for each path to evaluate your progress and impact. Finally, set a timeline for reassessment to ensure your chosen path is delivering value.

Executive Path Decision Framework

To help clarify your decision, this decision path might help you.

Career Timeline Assessment

There is no absolute path. Although we have used the idea of "less than 5 years" or "more than ten years" to help direct the flowchart, these are suggestions. Indeed, some may embark on the REWIRE path for a few years and then opt to shift into the RETIRE Path. So, this is very much a framework to help prompt your thinking and where we believe the strong indicators might be to choose one path or the other.

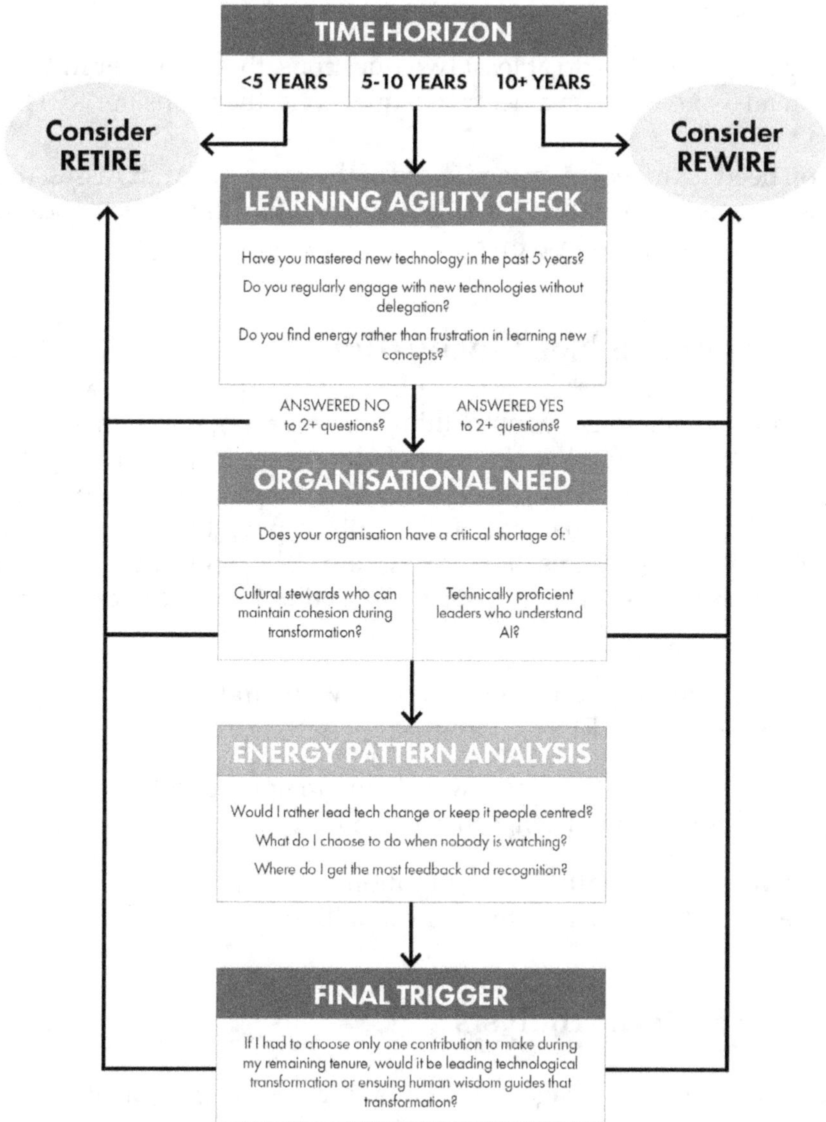

If your timeline is 5–10 years, then we urge you to assess your learning agility:

- Have you mastered significant new technical domains in the past 5 years?
- Do you regularly engage directly with new technologies without delegation?
- Do you find energy rather than frustration in learning technical concepts?

If you answered 'Yes' to at least two questions, then consider REWIRE. If you answered 'No' to at least two questions, then consider RETIRE.

If you need to do more work on some of these areas, our dQ assessment tools and learning paths can help you consider those gaps and how quickly you want to close them.

Organisational Need Evaluation

We would encourage you to think of your organisation's current position. What would happen if all of your peers on your management team opted for retirement? Do you have enough talent in depth, and do you have enough balance of the skills, capabilities and mindset to really exploit the organisation's "rewiring?". To begin with, start with yourself and asses whether your organisation have a critical shortage of:

- Technically proficient leaders who understand AI? Then consider REWIRE
- Cultural stewards, who can maintain cohesion during transformation? Then, consider RETIRE

Align your choice with the organisation's more pressing gap unless it fundamentally conflicts with your capabilities.

Energy Pattern Analysis

We would also encourage you to monitor your engagement during a two-week period:

- Track your energy level when engaged in technical learning vs. human development activities
- Note which activities you naturally prioritise when given the choice
- Identify which contributions generate the most positive feedback

Your natural energy patterns often reveal your authentic path more reliably than intellectual analysis alone.

Final Decision Trigger

If multiple indicators point to different paths, ask yourself: "If I had to choose only one contribution to make during my remaining tenure, would it be leading technological transformation or ensuring human wisdom guides that transformation?"

Your immediate, intuitive response often reveals your true priority.

What distinguishes successful executives isn't which path they choose but their willingness to make an explicit choice rather than defaulting to inaction. The worst position is attempting to straddle both paths without committing to either.

Throughout this book we have emphasised that AI is a leadership issue not a technology one, and so if your uncertainty is based on whether you need to understand the technology, our advice is to focus less on the technology, and being able to understand its intended use, and focus on making sure you know how to ask the right questions, and understand the consequences of the answers. Both paths require that human judgment.

General Sir Nick Carter summed it up as this: "There's a big distinction in the modern working life between being an intelligent customer of technology and being a technologist. And what people like you and I have got to become is an intelligent customer of technologies so that I can ask the right questions".

Recognising Warning Signs

If you've chosen the REWIRE path but keep avoiding hands-on learning or find yourself stuck in abstraction, pause. You may be forcing a direction that doesn't serve you.

If you've chosen the RETIRE path but feel like you're being left out or irrelevant in key conversations, it might be time to step closer to the centre of the change.

Pay attention to your energy. Fatigue, irritation, and quiet disengagement are clues.

Sir Martin Sorrell, founder of WPP and later S4 Capital, shared his experience in a 2024 Campaign interview: "I initially tried to combine my traditional leadership style with becoming a digital pioneer. It was exhausting and ineffective. When I launched S4, I made a different choice—I surrounded myself with digital natives while focusing on my strengths in client relationships and strategic vision. That clarity of purpose made all the difference."

Moving Forward

When Alan Jope made his decision at Unilever, he didn't simply step back. He created a deliberate transition plan that included establishing a digital advisory board, pairing senior leaders with technical mentors, and building AI literacy requirements into succession planning. His choice wasn't about disengagement; it was about purposeful focus.

Similarly, when Luis Gallego at IAG committed to the REWIRE path, he created accountability structures around his learning journey, including quarterly reviews with his board on how his developing digital fluency was shaping the company's strategy.

The hardest part of all this isn't understanding all of the concepts and insights in this book; it's the decision to lead yourself first. Be honest about your capability, appetite, and ambition, and act accordingly.

To make your choice count:

- ***Communicate your decision.*** Let key stakeholders know which path you've chosen and why

- ***Create accountability structures.*** Build mechanisms that keep you committed to your chosen direction

- ***Establish clear success metrics.*** Define what progress looks like on your chosen path

- ***Review regularly.*** Set quarterly check-ins to assess whether your choice is serving both you and your organisation

- ***Model transparency.*** Make your learning journey visible to others, regardless of which path you choose

What matters isn't whether you take the REWIRE or the RETIRE path. What matters is that you've chosen it with care and, in doing so, made space for others to do the same.

Leadership in the age of AI isn't about becoming something you're not. It's about becoming more of what your organisation needs, at exactly the moment it matters most.

Chapter 12

REWIRE YOUR LEADERSHIP STYLE

You've taken the assessment. You've seen the score. Now comes the part that's harder to quantify—what you do with it.

If you've chosen the REWIRE path, this chapter is your guide. You're already leading teams, making high-stakes decisions, and navigating complexity. But now you're facing something more personal: how do I lead when the very idea of leadership is being rewritten around me?

The first point is that everyone's REWIRE journey will be different. There will be those who take it slowly, who perhaps are more tentative and still need some convincing. There will be others that have leapt in with both feet and are eager to start. For these reasons, we have deliberately written this chapter—and the subsequent RETIRE chapter — in a slightly different style to the rest of this book.

We have adopted a more provocative and action-focused approach to encourage you to step back, think and make your own plan. We also want to provide tangible advice to help you start your journey. If you want a more structured and prescriptive way of starting your REWIRE journey, we have produced a simple workbook with different advice for the various levels of dQ that you might have achieved. Here, we seek to provoke some ideas, illicit suggestions, and provide space for reflection. We leave how you act on that up to you.

Let's break down the details behind the REWIRE mnemonic that we introduced in the previous chapter.

REWIRE CONTINUOUS CYCLE

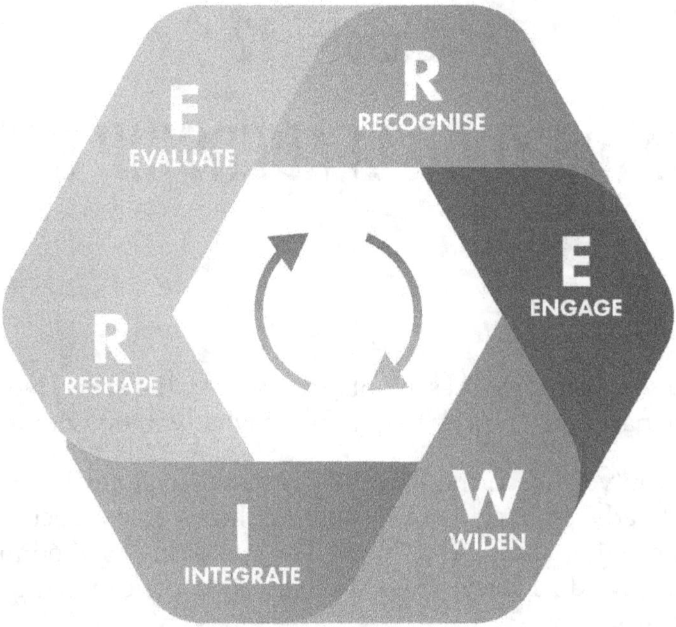

Recognise

This is where the rewiring begins—with recognition. Not the polished version of where you think you are, but the honest one of where you actually are. Because in times of change, especially with something as complex as AI, the hardest truths to see are often the ones closest to home.

Recognition here isn't about admitting failure. It's about clearing away the fog that tends to build around senior roles. The longer you've led, the more you're at risk of mistaking awareness for understanding. You've heard the updates. You've sponsored a pilot. Maybe your team even briefed you on how AI is being applied. But how much of that is deep engagement, and how much is performance? It's a confronting question—but a necessary one.

Start with yourself. What do you truly understand about how AI is being used in your own organisation? Not the theory—your people already have access to that. The practical. Could you explain, in plain language, how a tool like ChatGPT works and where its limits lie? Have you explored how it might change how your team solves problems, communicates, or makes decisions? Have you used any of these tools yourself, not just to observe, but to notice how they shift your own thinking?

Then look at your mindset. What story are you carrying, often unconsciously, about this wave of change? Are you hoping AI is just a passing trend, something your more technical colleagues will deal with while you stay focused on 'bigger' leadership matters? Or do you believe your experience, gut instinct, and judgment, honed over decades, are enough to lead effectively, regardless of the tools around you?

None of these beliefs is irrational. But each one, if left unexamined, can quietly narrow your vision at the exact moment it needs to widen.

Now, shift the lens to your team. Are you assuming they're more fluent than you? Or perhaps that they're waiting for your permission to explore? Have you created enough psychological space for experimentation, or are people watching you for cues and seeing that curiosity is optional?

And then, the organisation. Where is AI already in play, quietly changing how things get done? In customer service flows? In forecasting? In vendor selection? Often, the most significant shifts happen under the radar. If you haven't gone looking, you won't know. And if you don't know, you can't lead.

This kind of recognition is often more about posture than knowledge. Are you open? Defensive? Dismissive? Quietly overwhelmed? None of these are fixed states. They're signals—clues about where your growth needs to begin.

This isn't about shame. Or urgency for its own sake. It's about clarity. Because when you know where you're standing, you can choose where to step next. And leadership—authentic leadership—begins with that choice.

So, find an hour. No meetings, no distractions. Ask yourself: What am I avoiding? What do I genuinely understand? What part of this landscape feels unfamiliar, and what would I need to feel more confident? Write it down.

Then go and talk to someone in your organisation who's close to this work. Don't ask for a report. Ask for a conversation. What are they trying? What's breaking? What's more complicated than it looked? Listen. Learn. Let it unsettle you, if it needs to.

Because the most credible leaders I've seen in this space are not the ones who pretend to know—they're the ones who identify their uncomfortable knowledge gaps and are willing to fill them.

Engage

Recognition without engagement changes nothing. It gives you insight, but no momentum. And in a world being reshaped by AI, awareness isn't enough. You have to move, even if that movement is hesitant at first.

Engagement here doesn't mean signing off on a roadmap or delegating to a capable team. It means stepping into the experience yourself—directly, personally, without the usual filters of reports and second-hand summaries. It means getting closer to the thing you're being asked to lead.

And that's uncomfortable for many senior leaders. You're used to shaping direction, not handling the tools. You've earned the right to operate at altitude, yet this feels like returning to ground level. But leadership doesn't live in abstraction. Not anymore. Not here.

You don't need to become an expert. You don't need to code. You need to engage deliberately and repeatedly with the tools that are changing how your people work, decide, and collaborate.

Start small. Choose one tool and try it, not as a test, but as part of your work. Use it to draft a note, rethink a comms plan, or review a document. Then pause and ask: How did that feel? What came easily? What surprised you? What made you uncomfortable? Where did it fall short?

This isn't about evaluating the tool. It's about observing yourself and how your thinking shifts when a system offers suggestions. Do you defer? Do you edit? Do you resist?

Because that's where the real insight lies—not in the technology, but in your response to it.

The leaders who make the strongest impact in this space aren't the ones who know the most. They're the ones who are willing to try, who are open about what they're learning, who model curiosity, and who make it safe for others to experiment.

When your team sees that you're engaged, not just interested, they start to believe that change isn't something being done to them. It's something they're part of. They'll try more, share more, and think differently.

And that's where momentum builds.

It helps to create a regular habit. We suggest you block thirty minutes each week to explore something new: a tool, a use case, or a shift in how someone on your team approaches their work. You don't need to have an agenda; just turn up with an interest and an open mind. Keep a simple log—what you tried, what you noticed, what you're wondering. It's not a performance but a practice.

And yes, you'll make mistakes. You'll misunderstand how something works, or you'll feel slow. That's the point. It puts you back in the learner's seat and reminds you what it feels like to be unsure. And from that place, you'll lead with more empathy and more relevance.

You'll also begin to see things others miss. You will notice the frictions in different processes, the opportunities to redesign or the places where a little automation could free up a lot of attention. This engagement will sharpen your ability to see clearly, not just what's changing, but what's possible.

And if you ever find yourself thinking, "This isn't really for me," that's precisely the moment to re-engage. Because the people watching you are still deciding whether this is real. And your posture—more than your policies—will shape what they do next.

So don't wait for certainty or the perfect moment. Pick something and try it. Then talk about it, and do it all over again.

You're not here to master the machines. You're here to lead the humans who will work alongside them. And that begins with stepping in, not staying back.

Widen

By now, you've stepped in. You've started using a few tools, tested the waters, maybe even shifted how you approach specific tasks. You've built enough familiarity to see that this isn't a passing trend, but you also know you're still seeing only part of the picture.

That's precisely why this stage matters. Widening is about expanding your view beyond the immediate and obvious. Because early engagement, while essential, is often limited by proximity. You explore what's relevant to your role, what others have recommended, and what feels within reach. That's a good start. But if you stay in that comfort zone, you risk mistaking familiarity for understanding.

Widening means deliberately moving beyond your usual frame, looking across functions, industries, geographies, even generations, to gain a broader sense of how AI is actually being used, tested, questioned, and adapted. And just as importantly, how it's reshaping expectations around value, speed, and human input.

This isn't about trend-spotting. It's about recalibrating your lens so you can lead with sharper judgment.

You might hear about the same AI tool being applied in wildly different ways: a law firm using it to summarise case notes, a marketing team generating campaign variants at scale, a logistics provider optimising routes in real time. Each use case offers a signal, not just about technology, but about leadership. About what becomes possible when constraints are challenged.

And that's the shift. You stop asking, "How does this apply to us?" and start asking, "What if it did?" or "What would it take for us to operate that way?" It's a move from observation to imagination.

To do this well, you must be willing to feel out of place. You must read things that aren't written for people like you or join events where you're not the most experienced voice in the room. You might want to try following conversations that don't feed your existing beliefs. The aim isn't to find perfect answers—it's to stretch the way you think.

Some leaders make this a formal habit: setting up monthly conversations with people outside their industry, shadowing different functions within the business, or asking junior staff to talk them through the tools they use and how those tools shape their thinking. The point isn't to become an expert in everything. It's to notice the assumptions you didn't realise you were making.

And it's not just about looking outwards. Widening also means noticing what's happening quietly within your own organisation. Who's experimenting informally? Who's pushing the boundaries of their role, trying out tools that haven't yet been officially sanctioned? These are often your early signals—your internal edge cases. Pay attention and support them. Engage with those colleagues and ask them what they're learning.

Because when your perspective broadens, your questions change. You move from "Are we using AI?" to "Where are we stuck in outdated patterns?" From "What's the return on this tool?" to "What new behaviours are starting to emerge?" That shift in question often signals a shift in leadership maturity.

By now, you're no longer chasing certainty, but learning to lead with curiosity—systematically, not sporadically. And from that posture, you're better placed to help others navigate uncertainty, too.

So widen your lens—not to gather more information but to build more perspective. The next phase will demand that.

Integrate

This is the moment when the rewiring begins to shape not just how you think but also how your organisation operates. Integration is where early experiments give way to fundamental shifts—where AI moves off the whiteboard and into workflows. It's where leadership is most visible because this is where decisions start to carry weight.

Up to now, you've been learning, testing, and absorbing. You've tried tools, listened with genuine curiosity to the voices around you, and perhaps even reimagined how a process or two might be improved. But integration will demand more. It asks you to connect that early exploration to your organisation's lived reality—to move from "what's possible" to "what changes."

Many leaders hesitate here, not because they don't believe in the opportunity, but because integration introduces risk. It forces decisions: What tools do we embed? Where do we pilot? Who do we involve? How do we maintain clarity and trust while the ground shifts beneath people's feet?

It's tempting to wait—to gather more data, form more committees, run more low-stakes experiments. But too much caution signals indecision. People start to doubt whether change is real. They wait for permission instead of acting with intent. That's when progress stalls.

The challenge is to lead with enough clarity to give direction and enough flexibility to allow adaptation. That means choosing a few high-value areas where AI could enhance performance or reduce friction and backing those choices with visible support, not from the sidelines but with involvement—framing the why, clarifying expectations, and holding space for both ambition and uncertainty.

It also means being honest about the human side. Integration isn't just a systems upgrade. It touches roles, routines, and relationships. It creates tension. Some people will resist, others will overpromise, and most will feel uncertain—sometimes all in the same week. Your role is to make sense of that tension, not eliminate it, to hold the space where progress and discomfort can coexist.

Clarity matters here. Be explicit about what's changing, what's not, and what you're still figuring out. Tell people where AI is intended to support their judgment, not override it. Define the boundaries early: where the tool leads, where the human leads, and how the two interact. Without that clarity, people either retreat into old habits or overcorrect in ways that create new risks.

You'll also need new metrics. Efficiency might improve, but at what cost? Does decision quality hold? Does confidence grow or falter? Are the gains in speed matched by gains in understanding? Make sure you pay attention to the quieter signals—who stops contributing, who feels sidelined, who's energised and why. The cultural impact of integration often precedes the measurable one.

And then, keep listening. Integration is not a one-time event but a series of adaptations—some planned, many reactive. You won't get it all right. But the leaders who make this work are the ones who notice, adjust, and stay present. They don't wait for the quarterly review. They ask weekly: What's working? What's getting in the way? What needs to be rethought?

We talked with one CEO who ran a daily five-minute pulse check for a month after launching an AI-enhanced planning process. It was not a performance review; just a check-in. She asked just one question: "What surprised you today?" The insights that surfaced shaped the next phase more effectively than any external consultant could have. That's what leadership looks like mid-integration—curious, responsive, grounded.

We said earlier in this book that AI is all about leadership, not technology, and integration will stall if it is only about the latter. Yet, it will take hold if it becomes about how people learn to think, decide, and collaborate differently.

This isn't about automating your organisation. It's about weaving in new capabilities with care, so that people feel equipped, not replaced.

And it's about setting the tone that this isn't optional, but it's not reckless either. We're doing this together, and we're doing it thoughtfully.

Get that right, and integration won't be an initiative. It will become the way your organisation evolves.

Reshape

This is the point where leadership starts to stretch, not just in how you lead but in what you choose to lead toward. Up until now, you've been learning, experimenting, and integrating new ideas and tools. But reshaping means taking a harder, deeper look at your organisation's underlying logic. It's about asking—not just how we adapt—but whether we need to rethink what we're aiming for altogether.

Many leaders stop short of this step. They make improvements. They modernise. They digitise. But they don't thoroughly question the assumptions that sit beneath their business model, their operating rhythms, or their value proposition. Often, that hesitation comes from success. When what you've built still works, even partially, it's hard to ask whether it should be rebuilt.

But in a world reshaped by AI, the limits that used to define your strategy—scale, speed, human expertise, physical reach—are being renegotiated. And that creates a different kind of responsibility. The question isn't just how you can do things better. It's whether you're still doing the right things at all.

So, at this point, we suggest you take a step back, not from your team or your targets, but from your defaults. Ask yourself: What part of our organisation depends on complexity that AI can now simplify? What part depends on scale that's no longer an advantage? What decisions are being treated as strategic but are increasingly automated, commoditised, or irrelevant?

This kind of reflection isn't easy. It can feel disloyal to past strategies, successful playbooks, or even your own leadership story. But reshaping isn't about throwing everything out. It's about letting go of what no longer serves and making space for what could.

Start with one thread. Maybe it's a customer journey that feels clunky, a process that creates bottlenecks or a product that assumes scarcity where there is now abundance. Use AI not just to improve what's there, but to reimagine what's possible.

We've seen organisations take this step in different ways. One used AI to cut weeks out of its new client onboarding process—then used that time not to push harder, but to build better early relationships with clients. Another revisited its pricing model entirely, shifting from time-based billing to outcome-based value. In both cases, the shift wasn't just about the tech. It was about what the tech made thinkable.

Sometimes, reshaping is about role and identity. Leaders who once defined themselves by oversight now become enablers; some who identified as experts become guides, while others who were gatekeepers now become translators. The question becomes: What's my value now, and where is it most needed?

This isn't a single pivot. It's a mindset. A willingness to return to first principles. To ask what kind of organisation you would build today, if legacy systems, legacy logic, or legacy roles didn't constrain you.

It doesn't mean rushing toward disruption for its own sake. It means creating space to imagine a better version of what you already do—and trusting your team to help shape it. Often, they've seen the cracks already. They're just waiting for the invitation to do something about them.

So pause, reflect, and challenge your assumptions. Then, take one meaningful step—not to abandon the past but to reshape what the future could be if you stopped treating the present as permanent.

Evaluate

If there's a centre of gravity in the REWIRE journey, this is it. Evaluation isn't the last step. It's the rhythm that keeps the others alive. Without it, recognition fades, engagement becomes sporadic, and integration risks drifting into habit rather than direction. Evaluation is what keeps your leadership intentional in a world that moves faster than your calendars can keep up.

And it starts with you.

Most senior leaders are well-practised at reviewing performance in others. You're used to assessing plans, budgets, and outcomes. But this is different. This is about reviewing your own leadership posture. Not to score yourself, but to stay in motion. To ask: Is what I'm learning actually changing how I lead?

Set time aside to reflect—not once a year, but regularly. No slide decks, no performance metrics—just questions. What assumptions have I let go of? Where have I stepped into discomfort recently? What am I hearing from my teams that I might not have listened to a year ago? These aren't soft reflections. They're strategic checks. Because if you're not evolving, neither is your organisation.

But evaluation isn't just a solo exercise. It needs feedback from your peers, from your direct reports, and even from the people you rarely hear from unless something goes wrong. Ask them what's shifted or what still feels abstract, unreal or embryonic to them. Ask them what's been said but not yet lived. If you create the space—and genuinely listen—you'll get insight that no dashboard can offer.

You must also look outward, not to benchmark, but to sense patterns. What are your competitors starting to prioritise? What tools are showing up in customer interactions, not just internal pilots? What's becoming normal elsewhere that still feels novel in your world? These signals aren't distractions but part of the context that your leadership now operates within.

And then there's the uncomfortable part—acknowledging what didn't work. The tool that fell flat, the initiative that didn't scale or the moments where AI felt more like friction than freedom. These aren't failures to hide, but data to use to learn and improve. And if you don't extract the learning, you risk repeating the waste.

The most adaptive leaders we've spoken to don't ask, "Did it succeed?" They ask, "What did we learn—and what does that change about what we do next?" That shift—from proving to improving—creates the psychological safety that teams need to keep trying, sharing, and learning.

Make this curiosity visible. Build light-touch rituals that reinforce learning. It could be as simple as a retrospective, a team debrief or a short, structured reflection at the end of a pilot. Not just "what happened," but "what surprised us?" and "what do we do differently now?"

Over time, this kind of evaluation becomes cultural. It moves out of the leadership suite and into teams' daily rhythms. And that's the goal—not perfection, but progress, not activity, but awareness.

Because this isn't a one-time journey, REWIRE is not a single circuit—it's a continuous loop. When you recognise something new, you engage again, widen your view, and integrate more confidently. You reshape your thinking and direction by asking bolder questions, and then you evaluate—not just the work, but the thinking behind it.

And you begin again. That's the habit that keeps your leadership alive, alert, relevant, and capable of meeting change with clarity, rather than just coping with it.

You've chosen to REWIRE. This is how you stay rewired.

The Continuous Learning Loop

The REWIRE framework isn't linear—it's cyclical. As you evaluate, you'll recognise new gaps. As you reshape, you'll need to engage with new tools. Each element reinforces the others, creating a continuous learning loop that evolves with your organisation and the technology landscape.

What matters most isn't perfection at any stage but momentum through all of them. The leaders who thrive with AI aren't those who understand every technical detail—they're those who adapt their leadership approach to a world where technology and human judgment increasingly intertwine.

Your score isn't a final grade. It's the starting point of a leadership journey that will continually evolve. Begin where you are—with one recognition, one engagement, one widened perspective. The rest will follow.

As you progress through REWIRE, you'll notice a shift in your leadership focus. You will spend less time on tasks that AI can handle well and pay more attention to questions humans can answer better. Less concern about operational details. More clarity about the strategic direction. This shift doesn't diminish leadership—it elevates it to where it belongs.

In the end, the REWIRE framework isn't about technology at all. It's about leadership adaptability in a changing world. It's where you stop reacting to change and start responding to it—with agility, intent, judgement, and a clear view of what comes next.

Chapter 13

RETIRE AND KEEP INVOLVED

Some leaders run forward. Others guide from the side. If you're reading this chapter, you've likely chosen the latter. Not because you lack ambition or energy, but because you recognise where your true value lies.

The RETIRE path is not about stepping away from leadership or surrendering to technological change. It's about a deliberate choice to lead differently, drawing on your human experience at precisely the time when it matters most. As AI shifts how organisations operate, the wisdom of lived leadership becomes more valuable, not less. But the role changes. You become the stabiliser, the translator, and the guide who ensures progress doesn't come at the cost of people, values, or organisational cohesion.

When you completed your Digital Intelligence (dQ) assessment, you may have made a clear-eyed evaluation that the REWIRE path wasn't right for you. Perhaps the timeline of your career makes deep AI immersion impractical. Perhaps your strengths and motivations align more naturally with human-centred leadership than technological transformation. Whatever your reasoning, you've chosen a path that has equal value but a different focus.

What follows is your roadmap for this journey—a structured approach to redefining your contribution, amplifying your influence, and creating lasting impact in an era of profound technological change. As with chapter 12, we ask provocative questions to inspire you to reflect hard on how you will stay relevant and valuable as a leader. The RETIRE framework provides six practical stages that will guide your evolution. Unlike the cyclical nature of the REWIRE framework, the RETIRE process is more linear—not exclusively so, there may well be sections you redo, or decide to rethink, but broadly this is a sequential process.

RETIRE PHASES

Each component offers practical guidance for staying impactful, relevant and distinctly human during a time of unprecedented technological disruption. Let's explore how you can leverage your experience to provide the leadership that AI-driven organisations desperately need.

Redirect Focus

This isn't about retreating from relevance. It's about moving with intention—choosing where your insight matters most in an organisation that's shifting faster than it can sometimes process. Redirecting your focus is the first act in leading with longevity in mind, not legacy.

Start with this: where does your experience add value that no tool can replicate well? That's not a rhetorical question. It's the point. AI is advancing faster each month, but it still can't replicate the judgment of a seasoned leader, built upon years (decades even) of hard decisions, long-term consequences, and lived contradictions. You've made trade-offs others haven't even considered yet. That perspective is your differentiator.

But the reality is, the more senior you've become, the more you're pulled into oversight and away from impact. Redirecting your focus means identifying what only you can contribute, and having the discipline to say no to what others can handle.

So, where do you begin? With clarity. Look for the conversations where your insight reshapes the thinking. So, for example, perhaps you've been valued for how to best influence and persuade others in your organisation to a new approach, where the subtleties of power and egos need to be considered carefully. Notice where people lean in and reflect on the decisions where you brought perspective, not just approval. These are not always in your job description, but they are the work only you can do.

There's also an act of letting go here. You don't need to track every AI trend. You don't have to master the tools. You need to understand enough to ask better questions, recognise implications others might miss, and shape priorities from the perspective of someone who understands more than metrics.

One experienced COO we talked to used to run the numbers in every board meeting. Then they stopped and instead, focused their contribution on interpreting what the numbers didn't say—what had shifted, what historical context mattered, what unseen risks might surface. They hadn't stepped back; they had stepped into something far more valuable.

Redirecting also means resisting distraction. There's no prize for being across everything, so focus instead on where your insight carries the most weight. Choose two or three areas that truly matter to your organisation's future and show up there with clarity, consistency and calm.

This isn't about doing less. It's about showing up where your judgment stretches others' thinking, where your presence reassures, and where your voice makes the next step feel clearer.

If that sounds simple, it isn't. But it's doable, and it starts with acknowledging that your role now isn't to run faster. It's to steady the course.

Empower Others

If redirecting your focus is a personal choice, empowering others is a relational one. It's the act of handing over—not just responsibilities, but belief. It's not something you do once at the end. It's something you do repeatedly, patiently, and deliberately while you're still in the room.

You've accumulated sound judgment experience over the years, perhaps decades. But that's only useful to the organisation if it's transferred, not hoarded. Empowering others means recognising that your legacy isn't what you finish—it's what others are able to start because of you.

This requires a shift in mindset. You're not looking for the next version of yourself. You're not searching for someone who leads or thinks the way you do. You're identifying the people who are already shaping the future and deciding to invest your energy in helping them lead with greater clarity and confidence.

That might mean mentoring someone outside your function who doesn't yet see themselves as a leader but who others instinctively look to. It might mean stepping aside in a meeting so a quieter voice can shape the conversation. Or it might be about naming potential before the person sees it in themselves and sticking with them long enough that they believe it.

The most powerful leaders we've seen in transition build informal networks of influence. They create circles of trust, but they don't wait to be asked—they reach out. They invite early-career leaders to shadow them. They make space for different perspectives. They choose curiosity over critique.

This isn't a soft skill. It's a strategic one.

Because the most significant risk in times of change isn't technical failure, it's a lack of leadership confidence—a vacuum of judgment. A generation coming through without a clear sense of how to think, weigh, and pause.

You can fill that gap—not by instructing, but by including.

Some of the most effective mentoring happens without ever being named as such. It's in the coffee chat that turns into a strategic conversation, in the story you share that reframes someone's situation, and in the act of being available when someone needs a sounding board and isn't quite sure who to ask.

Equally, this is a moment to listen differently. Reverse mentoring isn't just a useful concept—it's an essential context. Let someone younger show you the tools they use. Ask them how they make decisions, what they assume about work, and what feels natural to them. Not only will it sharpen your understanding, but it will also show them that your interest is real.

And interest is what makes people feel empowered. Not flattery. Not token gestures. Just the steady signal that you believe they're ready for more—and you're here to support, not to oversee.

So ask yourself: Who are you intentionally nurturing right now? Who have you backed publicly and coached privately? Who have you trusted with your thinking, not just your tasks?

Empowering others isn't about preparing to exit but choosing to matter differently. Your influence doesn't end when you step back from the centre. It expands when others step forward and carry something you helped build.

Translate Values

Values aren't abstract. They show up in moments of pressure. They guide decisions when the right choice isn't obvious. And in times of significant change, like the one AI now demands, those values must be translated and transmitted repeatedly so they stay useful.

This is where you offer something essential.

You've led through ambiguity. You've made decisions when the data wasn't precise, the stakes were high, and the consequences were yours to carry. You've felt the weight of choosing between speed and care, growth and trust, simplicity and integrity. Those decisions didn't just reflect your values. They shaped the organisation's memory of what leadership looks like.

But memories fade. And values, if not translated into new contexts, become slogans. That's why this part of your role matters more than ever—not as a guardian of the past, but as an interpreter for the present.

Translating values doesn't mean resisting change. It is partly about transmitting the values (because they have not changed, just the context in which they are used) and translating them because some colleagues will still need help to see the existing values in a new context, where much of the language around those values has changed. It means ensuring that, as the systems evolve, the organisation isn't carried away from what makes it recognisable to and trusted by the people within it, as well as other critical stakeholders. It means making sure that the questions people ask themselves—about fairness, impact, accountability—still lead them to the right conversations.

And it means making the implicit explicit. Don't assume that everyone sees the connection between the new way of doing things and the old principles you helped to shape. Spell it out and tell the story. Walk them through the why, not just the what.

We've worked with leaders who do this almost invisibly, adding a single sentence in a strategy session that anchors the room: "Let's not forget that speed here shouldn't come at the cost of consent." Or: "Remember, just because the model can do it, doesn't mean it should." These aren't grandstanding comments. They're quiet recalibrations. They remind people of the line between what's possible and what's right.

It also helps to bring the past into the room, not as nostalgia but as context. Talk about the time the organisation made the harder choice because it aligned with who you were trying to be. Use that story as a compass when people feel unsure. You're not holding things back; you're helping them steer.

And while you're doing that, be willing to challenge what's become performative. Sometimes, people defend a process or a phrase because it's "the way we've always done it," when in fact it's lost all real meaning. Part of your work is to clear away what no longer carries weight—and to protect what still does.

It's not always neat. Values won't always agree with each other. There'll be tensions between commercial pressure and ethical concern, between speed and reflection. You're not expected to resolve every conflict. But you are expected to ensure those tensions are acknowledged and discussed.

Because when they're not, people stop asking the more profound questions. And that's when the culture starts to drift.

So don't assume your values have already been embedded. Ask where they need updating. Ask where they're being quietly bypassed. And ask what they look like in this next phase—when the tools are different, but the people are still human.

You're not defending the past. You're translating what still matters into a language this future can understand.

Influence Strategy

Strategic influence changes shape as your formal responsibilities evolve. It becomes less about decision rights and more about decision quality. You may no longer be in every meeting, or hold the same remit you once did—but you now bring context, memory, and a well-trained eye for pattern and consequence. That's what strategy needs, even if the organisation doesn't always know it.

This isn't about being the loudest voice in the room. It's about asking the questions that sharpen the discussion. "What are we assuming?" "What could we be missing?" "What would this look like if we weren't protecting the existing model?" These aren't rhetorical, they are recalibrations—gentle, deliberate prompts that pull people out of their own functional blind spots.

And your timing matters. You've probably seen how fast things can run away from intention—when a strategic plan picks up speed and momentum but drifts from its original purpose. At this stage, influence often means stepping in just long enough to refocus. Not to take over or reroute everything, but to pause the room, to ask the question no one else is asking, and then let the group get back to work, slightly changed.

You bring not only experience but also a sense of proportion, which can be rare when a team is immersed in technical detail or pressured by quarterly targets. You offer the wide-angle lens, and when you use it well, you help teams shift from fixation to perspective—from urgency to alignment.

But this role also demands restraint. Influence that lands well is influence that is timed, thoughtful, and light of touch. It respects the energy of the room. It doesn't demand the spotlight. It doesn't interrupt to be heard. It listens until the moment to speak is obvious—and then it says the thing that needs to be said, clearly and without ego.

One seasoned leader we talked to described this phase as moving from "driver to compass". Not the one turning the wheel, but the one keeping direction true. Still vital, still felt, but quieter—and, in many ways, more powerful.

So, ask yourself: where is strategy actually being shaped? Who's doing the shaping? Are you in the right conversations? And when you are, are you helping people see further, or just think faster?

This kind of influence is subtle. But it sticks. In rooms where everyone is chasing answers, the person who reframes the question is often the one who leaves the deepest mark.

Reinforce Culture

Culture carries an organisation's emotional memory. It's the story people tell themselves about what really matters—who gets listened to, what gets rewarded, and how it feels to belong. In moments of significant change, that story either strengthens the organisation's resilience or unravels its coherence.

You know this already. You've seen cultures evolve, fracture, renew. And now, as AI and automation reshape not just what we do, but how we do it, your role is to keep the culture intact—not by freezing it in time, but by tending to what must endure.

Reinforcing culture isn't about protecting rituals for the sake of tradition. It's about clarifying the core behaviours and beliefs that make your organisation recognisable to itself, even as everything else moves. It means surfacing what's essential: the way people challenge ideas without fear, the trust that underpins cross-functional work, the sense of fairness in decision-making when stakes are high.

These things can easily slip when speed becomes the default. AI can accelerate everything, and so conversations shorten and context gets stripped away. And if you're not careful, decisions start to feel mechanical—technically correct, but culturally hollow. That's where you make the difference.

One of the most practical things you can do is slow the story down. Share examples. Remind people of how the organisation has made difficult choices in the past and what those moments revealed about who you are. Not to dwell—but to anchor.

We've worked with leaders who treat cultural moments as strategic interventions. They take time in town halls to highlight someone who stood up for a colleague or who challenged a decision with integrity. They make the intangible feel real. Because what gets noticed gets repeated. And what gets repeated becomes culture.

But reinforcing culture also means evolving it. Some rituals no longer fit, and some language has outlived its meaning. Your role isn't to protect what's outdated—it's to recognise what no longer serves and help replace it with something better.

That includes being honest about the tensions that technology brings. There will be moments when the drive for efficiency cuts across long-held ways of working, when data points challenge gut instinct, and when automation is celebrated but people feel displaced. These aren't problems to solve in isolation. They're moments to name and explore. Doing so helps culture grow around change, not against it.

And don't try to carry this work alone. Look for others who model the values without needing to be told. The people who make room for others, ask awkward questions, and help new joiners feel part of something bigger are the people to bring together. Let them lead, too.

Because in the end, culture isn't what we write down—it's what we embody. And if you can help shape the environment where that embodiment is visible, consistent, and human, you've done something lasting.

Your presence won't be measured by how loudly you insisted on values. It'll be measured by how confidently others live them, long after you've moved on.

Enable Transition

There comes a point in every leadership journey when continuing to hold the reins starts to matter less than ensuring they are ready to be passed on. This is not about exiting. It's about enabling continuity—and doing it with intention, clarity, and care.

Too many transitions happen by accident. A slow fade. An unclear handover. A quiet exit. But when you've spent a career shaping outcomes, guiding teams, and holding space for difficult decisions, the way you leave becomes part of your legacy. It deserves the same thought you gave to the work itself.

Enabling transition doesn't begin on your last day. It starts while you still have influence. It's about recognising what lives only in your head—and finding ways to make it accessible to others. That might mean documenting how certain decisions were made, sharing stories that explain why particular paths were chosen, or surfacing the assumptions that shaped your approach. These aren't handbooks—they're frameworks for judgment.

And then comes the relational work. Who will carry this forward? Not just one named successor, but a set of people who collectively hold the future. Transition isn't a single handover—it's a layered process of distributing insight, confidence, and permission. Bring those people into the fold. Invite their perspective. Give them space to ask their version of the hard questions.

You also need to shift how you show up. If you were the one driving the strategy, become the one who listens for drift. If you were the one making final calls, become the sounding board others trust to test their instincts. Influence doesn't vanish—it changes shape. And if you carry it with grace, your presence will remain long after your name disappears from the org chart.

One senior leader we had several conversations with likened it to moving from the front seat to the passenger side. "I can still read the map," she said, "but I've stopped reaching for the wheel." She hadn't disappeared. She'd simply made space.

And that's the point. The goal of transition isn't absence—it's continuity. It's making sure that what mattered most while you led doesn't vanish when you don't.

Moving Forward

So don't go quietly. Go clearly. Talk about what's ahead. Share what you've learned. Own your mistakes. Name your hopes. Let people see that leadership includes endings—and that endings, done well, create confidence rather than uncertainty.

And if you stay involved—on a board, as a mentor, as a sounding board—stay in your new lane. Offer your judgement, not your oversight. Be generous with your support, but careful not to overshadow. Trust that you've prepared others well.

Because the most significant sign of your leadership may not be what happened while you held the role, but what happens next.

RETIRE isn't a resignation. It's a redirection of your wisdom into a form that serves the future. And the future needs it.

You've helped shape what came before. Now, you shape what comes after.

Chapter 13
CONCLUSION

We started this book with a simple premise: the rise of advanced technologies is fundamentally changing what it means to lead, not just how we lead but who we are as leaders.

After speaking with more than a hundred leaders across every imaginable sector—from military generals to start-up founders, from CFOs to healthcare innovators—we've seen the same pattern repeat itself again and again. The leadership divide is growing—not between the technically brilliant and the technically ignorant, but between those who've made a conscious choice about their leadership path and those who remain stuck in indecision.

The most unsettling discovery wasn't the pace of technological change, though that's certainly breathtaking. It was the vast gap between what executives say about technology and what they actually do. So many leaders talk a good game about digital transformation while postponing their own personal evolution. They delegate understanding rather than developing it. They prioritise operational concerns over strategic exploration. They sit in technology meetings without truly engaging.

We get it. Feeling like a novice again is uncomfortable, especially when you've spent decades building expertise. It's tempting to think you can delegate this particular challenge to those with more technical backgrounds. And for a brief period, that might even work.

But not anymore. Not now.

The choice you face as a leader isn't whether to engage with these technologies—that ship has sailed. The choice is whether to do so with intention, clarity and purpose, or drift along, reacting to changes as they arrive, always a step behind the curve.

When we began our research, we expected to find a single path forward for leaders: build your digital capabilities, increase your fluency, and lead transformation from the front. Instead, we discovered two equally valuable but distinctly different paths: REWIRE and RETIRE.

The REWIRE path is about becoming fluent in these new technologies—not as a technical specialist but as a leader who can thoughtfully guide transformation. It's about being willing to experiment, build new capabilities, and reimagine what your organisation might become.

The RETIRE path is equally vital. It's about doubling down on your uniquely human leadership qualities—your judgement, ethical compass and ability to build cultures where people feel valued. It's about ensuring that organisations don't lose sight of their purpose and values as technology accelerates change.

Both paths are necessary. Both create value. But straddling them—trying to do a bit of both without committing to either—is increasingly untenable. It creates the illusion of progress while delivering neither the technological fluency of REWIRE nor the human-centred leadership of RETIRE.

What matters isn't which path you choose. What matters is that you choose at all. That you make an explicit, considered decision about where your contribution will be most valuable in the years ahead.

For us, this journey has been illuminating and, at times, humbling. We've seen leaders we deeply respect struggle with the pace of change, with the sense that the ground is shifting beneath their feet. We've watched others transform themselves and their organisations by embracing new possibilities without abandoning what makes them effective.

But most of all, we've seen the power of intentional choice. The leaders who thrive in this new landscape aren't necessarily the most technically skilled or the most naturally charismatic. They're the ones who've taken a clear-eyed look at their capabilities, interests and organisation's needs and made deliberate choices about where to focus their energy.

They're the ones who've recognised that continuing to sit on the fence, to hedge their bets, creates the very anxiety they're trying to avoid. By choosing a path—whether REWIRE or RETIRE—they create clarity for themselves and for everyone around them.

So, as we conclude, we ask you: Which path will you choose?

If you're drawn to REWIRE, commit to it fully. Set aside time each week to experiment with these technologies. Build a learning network that challenges and supports you. Find opportunities to apply new capabilities to real business problems. Don't just talk about transformation—embody it.

If RETIRE feels right for you, embrace it with equal conviction. Define your role as a steward of human wisdom in an age of accelerating change. Mentor the next generation of leaders. Stand up for values and principles that might otherwise get lost in the rush toward efficiency. Be the voice that asks not just "Can we?" but "Should we?"

What you cannot afford to do is nothing. The cost of indecision grows by the day.

In our collective decades of leadership experience, we've never seen a more consequential moment for executives to make conscious choices about their own development. The stakes are too high, the pace too rapid, for anything less than deliberate action.

We titled this book "REWIRE or RETIRE" not as an ultimatum but as an invitation—an invitation to take control of your leadership journey at a moment when many feel control slipping away. It's an invitation to clarity in a time of confusion and to purpose in a time of disruption.

The technologies will continue to evolve. The business landscape will continue to transform. But amidst all this change, one thing remains constant: the need for leaders who know who they are, what they stand for and how they create value.

You now have the frameworks, the insights and the guidance to make your choice. The rest is up to you. We wish you every success with whichever path you choose.

If you wish to discuss some of the issues, participate in some of the webinars or learn more about dQ and your own journey, please visit our website, https://geni.us/rewireorretire.

Marco Ryan & Alastair Lechler

London, May 2025

HOW ABOUT A REVIEW?

If your actions inspire others to dream more, learn more, do more and become more, you are a leader.
~ John Quincy Adams

We hope that you are finding the book useful. We suspect that there are many other leaders out there, who were like you used to be. Less experienced, needing answers, but not sure who or what to trust.

Most people do, in fact, judge a book by its cover (and its reviews). So here's our request to you as an amazing leader who we know is committed to helping others succeed.

Please help that leader by leaving this book a review.

It's remarkably hassle-free, it doesn't cost you anything, it will take about 60 seconds and your review really could help.

If you are on audible - hit the three dots in the top right of your device, click rate & review, then leave a few sentences about the book with a star rating.

If you are reading on kindle, iPad or other tablet, scroll to the bottom of the book, then swipe up and it will prompt a review for you. You can also just scan this QR code:

If for some reason these are not working for you, then go to Amazon and leave a review right on the book's page. Here's the link:

https://geni.us/rewire-or-retire

Thank you for doing that. It makes more of a difference to the next leader who may be considering whether to get this book than you realize.

Please do also explore some of the other books in the "Leadership Impact Series" - we shall continue to add new titles through out the year.

Thank you so much

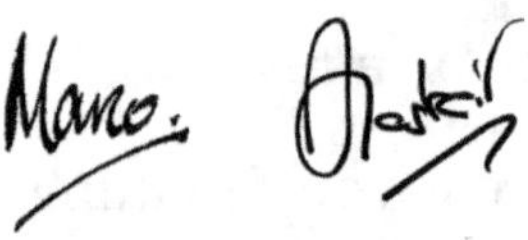

Marco and Alastair

London, May 2024

ABOUT THE AUTHORS

Marco Ryan

Marco has spent over two decades helping global companies make sense of digital change—leading strategies for data, AI, and transformation at firms like BP, Wärtsilä, and Thomas Cook. A former British Army officer, he built his leadership style in high-pressure environments long before stepping into C-suite roles.

Today, he advises executive teams on AI and cyber risk, coaches FTSE 100 board members, and teaches at Lancaster University Management School, where he's Cyber Leader in Residence. His books, including The Cybersecurity Blueprint and the 2024 series 101 Cyber Answers for Leaders, aim to make complex ideas practical for decision-makers.

A TEDx speaker and GCHQ-certified non-executive director, Marco also supports boards and mentors future leaders. He's been recognised by Forbes as a top digital voice—and continues to blend technical insight with a sharp focus on people and performance.

Alastair Lechler

Alastair is a Partner at Argon International, who bridges innovation with people-centred change. After surviving a 1000ft fall from a Scottish mountain in 2018, he embarked on a transformative sabbatical supporting aspiring startup founders through the Centre for Entrepreneurs. Alastair subsequently relocated to Edinburgh to launch ReBoot, a social enterprise focused on innovative outdoor coaching and development before linking the ReBoot model with Argon and returning to the corporate world.

Now with 25 years in executive recruitment and change leadership, Alastair is also a Fellow of the RSA and advocate for various charities including Protect Our Winters. His approach combines business transformation principles with experiential learning and teamship.

Alastair is a thought leader on culture change and the future of work - he emphasises purpose and wellbeing while advising leaders and organisations on building diverse teams capable of navigating complex change and innovation.

LEADERSHIP IMPACT SERIES

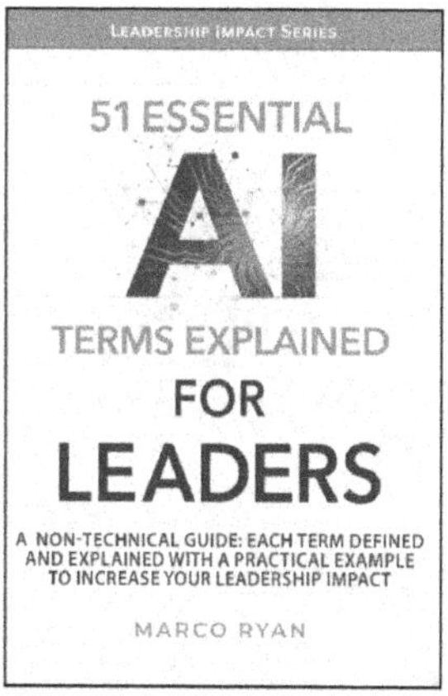

Other books in the series

RESOURCES

Christoforaki, M., & Beyan, O. (2022). AI Ethics—A Bird's Eye View. Applied Sciences, 12(9), 4130.

Vijai, C., & Wisetsri, W. (2021). Rise of Artificial Intelligence in Healthcare Startups in India. Advances in Management, 14(1), 48-52.

Kuzior, A., Kuzior, A., Sira, M., & Brożek, P. (2023). Use of Artificial Intelligence in Terms of Open Innovation Process and Management. Sustainability, 15(9), 7205.

Jancy, S. (2017, November 27). Creativity is the Next Economic Revolution. Scott Jancy. https://scottjancy.com/creativity-is-the-next-economic-revolution/

Szabó, K. (2018). Ramp-up process improvement practices for Time-to-Market reduction. Periodica Polytechnica Social and Management Sciences, 26(1), 19. https://doi.org/10.3311/ppso.9159

Gunasekara, S., & Saarela, M. (2025). Explainable AI in Education: Techniques and Qualitative Assessment. Applied Sciences, 15(3), 1239.

Decoding AI: Key terms for navigating the world of artificial intelligence. (n.d.). AiDebrief.com. https://www.aidebrief.com/articles/decoding-ai-key-terms-for-navigating-the-world-of-artificial-intelligence/

Developer. (2024, June 6). The AI Revolution: How Artificial Intelligence is Completely Changing Life as We Know It. https://technologyprofessionals.xyz/the-ai-revolution-how-artificial-intelligence-is-completely-changing-life-as-we-know-it/

Bryant, L. (n.d.). What is Digital Transformation, Digitalization, and Digitization | SHIFT*: Digital Capability Acceleration. https://

postshift.com/what-is-digital-transformation-digitalization-and-digitization/

Team, O. (2023, November 20). Unlocking the potential of AI-Powered software delivery solutions for enterprise success. OptimizDBA.com. https://optimizdba.com/unlocking-the-potential-of-ai-powered-software-delivery-solutions-for-enterprise-success/

Patil, R. (2024, September 17). 7 stages of AI adoption journey: Which milestone have you reached yet? Towards AI. https://towardsai.net/p/machine-learning/7-stages-of-ai-adoption-journey-which-milestone-have-you-reached-yet

Team, S. (2025, March 27). AI leadership: Why strong strategy matters. Scopic. https://scopicsoftware.com/blog/ai-leadership/

Tamayo, J., Doumi, L., Goel, S., Kovács-Ondrejkovic, O., & Sadun, R. (2023, September 1). Reskilling in the age of AI. Harvard Business Review. https://hbr.org/2023/09/reskilling-in-the-age-of-ai

The digital reinvention of an Asian Bank. (n.d.). DBS. https://www.dbs.com/media/digital-transformation/dbs-ceo-piyush-gupta-on-the-digital-reinvention-of-an-asian-bank.page

Zaytsev, A. (2024, October 19). Case study: Rio Tinto scales Machine learning for predictive maintenance, safety, and Sustainable operations. AIX | AI Expert Network. https://aiexpert.network/ai-at-rio-tinto/

8 key tips from NYT bestselling author Charlene Li on AI adoption and leadership. (n.d.). Nexthink. https://nexthink.com/blog/8-key-tips-from-nyt-bestselling-author-charlene-li-on-ai-adoption-and-leadership

Maybank - Digital Transformation Strategies. (2024, July 25). Market Research Reports & Consulting | GlobalData UK Ltd. https://www.globaldata.com/store/report/maybank-enterprise-tech-analysis/#:~:text=Maybank%20is%20leveraging%20AI%20and,platforms%20to%20support%20these%20capabilities.

Digital Literacy – DQ institute. (n.d.). https://www.dqinstitute.org/global-standards/

Digital Upskilling | Empower with the Right Digital Skills. (n.d.). Digitopia. https://digitopia.co/solutions/dq-digital-quotient/

Why employees are ready for AI but leaders are facing AI adoption challenges? | Mindflow Blog. (n.d.). https://mindflow.io/blog/why-employees-are-ready-for-ai-but-leaders-are-facing-challenges-with-ai-adoption

Massachusetts Institute of Technology. (2025, April 9). Why AI demands a new breed of leaders | MIT Sloan Management Review. MIT Sloan Management Review. https://sloanreview.mit.edu/article/why-ai-demands-a-new-breed-of-leaders/

Analytics, W. S. (2024, January 19). Data quality and impact on AI. https://www.linkedin.com/pulse/data-quality-impact-ai-wisdomschema-mw3dc

DeepMind AI reduces Google data centre cooling bill by 40%. (2025, April 24). Google DeepMind. https://deepmind.com/blog/article/deepmind-ai-reduces-google-data-centre-cooling-bill-40

Koningstein, R. (2021, May 19). We now do more computing where there's cleaner energy. Google. https://blog.google/outreach-initiatives/sustainability/carbon-aware-computing-location/

Google Cloud Blog. (n.d.). Google Cloud Blog. https://cloud.google.com/blog/products/infrastructure/google-data-centers-achieve-25-percent-higher-efficiency-through-advanced-ai-control-systems

Microsoft finds underwater datacenters are reliable, practical and use energy sustainably - Source. (2023, July 24). Source. https://news.microsoft.com/source/features/sustainability/project-natick-underwater-datacenter/

Considering Generative AI's environmental impact – MIT Climate & Sustainability Consortium. (2025, January 17). https://impactclimate.mit.edu/2025/01/17/considering-generative-ais-environmental-impact/

United Nations Environment Programme. (n.d.). AI has an environmental problem. Here's what the world can do about that.

UNEP. https://www.unep.org/news-and-stories/story/ai-has-environmental-problem-heres-what-world-can-do-about

Ltd, R. a. M. (n.d.-b). AXA - Digital Transformation Strategies - Research and Markets. Research and Markets Ltd 2025. https://www.researchandmarkets.com/reports/5702991/axa-digital-transformation-strategies

World Economic Forum. Future of Jobs Report 2023. Geneva: World Economic Forum Publications. https://www.weforum.org/publications/the-future-of-jobs-report-2023/

How AI changes your workforce | MIT Sloan Management Review. (2024, March 28). MIT Sloan Management Review. https://sloanreview.mit.edu/video/how-ai-changes-your-workforce/

Report - The digital transformation imperative. (n.d.). siemens.co.uk. https://www.siemens.com/uk/en/company/transform/reports.html

Putting the AI in audit. (2024, November 18). Deloitte United Kingdom. https://www.deloitte.com/uk/en/about/story/impact/putting-the-ai-in-audit.html

Gartner: Top strategic predictions for 2025 and beyond. (n.d.). https://get.nice.com/Gartner-2025-Trends

Shrestha, Yash & Ben-Menahem, Shiko & Krogh, Georg. (2019). Organizational Decision-Making Structures in the Age of Artificial Intelligence. California Management Review. 61. 000812561986225. 10.1177/0008125619862257. https://analyticsinstitute.edu.au/ikea-casestudy/

Chui, M., Hall, B., Mayhew, H., Singla, A., & Sukharevsky, A. (2022, December 6). The state of AI in 2022—and a half decade in review. McKinsey & Company. https://www.mckinsey.com/capabilities/quantumblack/our-insights/the-state-of-ai-in-2022-and-a-half-decade-in-review

TotalEnergies. (2023). March 2023 – Strategy, Sustainability & Climate. https://totalenergies.com/system/files/documents/2023-03/2023_

TotalEnergies_Strategy_Sustainability_Climate_Presentation.pdf

Tamayo, J., Doumi, L., Goel, S., Kovács-Ondrejkovic, O., & Sadun, R. (2023b, September 1). Reskilling in the age of AI. Harvard Business Review. https://hbr.org/2023/09/reskilling-in-the-age-of-ai

People matters global - Interstitial site — People matters global. (n.d.). People Matters. https://www.peoplemattersglobal.com/article/leadership/in-the-age-of-ai-goodbye-middle-managers-43723

Unilever. (2021). Unilever Future of Work Summit Report. https://www.unilever.com/files/9d3d2764-8a02-4af5-a287-f77f06ef4c5c/unilever-future-of-work-summit-report--4-.pdf

AI Assistant Startups funded by Y Combinator (YC) 2025 | Y Combinator. (n.d.). Y Combinator. https://www.ycombinator.com/companies/industry/ai-assistant

Vodafone Group Plc. (n.d.). Vodafone Group Plc Annual Report 2023. In Vodafone Group Plc Annual Report 2023. https://investors.vodafone.com/sites/vodafone-ir/files/2023-05/vodafone-fy23-annual-report.pdf

Plc, U. (2023, September 7). Alan Jope reflects on his time as Unilever CEO. Unilever. https://www.unilever.co.uk/news/2023/alan-jope-reflects-on-his-time-as-unilever-ceo/

Harvard Business Review. (2023). "C-Suite Confidence in the Digital Era." HBR Research Report, September 2023.

How a legacy financial institution went all in on Gen AI ^ H08O7O. (n.d.). HBR Store. https://store.hbr.org/product/how-a-legacy-financial-institution-went-all-in-on-gen-ai/H08O7O?sku=H08O7O-PDF-ENG

How Gen AI could change the value of expertise ^ H08MTC. (n.d.). HBR Store. https://store.hbr.org/product/how-gen-ai-could-change-the-value-of-expertise/h08mtc?fromSkuRelated=H08O7O&ab=store_idp_relatedpanel_-_how_gen_ai_could_change_the_value_of_expertise_H08MTC

Wood, D. (2024, November 29). IAG has 150 Gen AI "activators" across the company. Insurance Business UK. https://www.insurancebusinessmag.com/uk/news/technology/iag-has-150-gen-ai-activators-across-the-company-515926.aspx

Statement, D. C. (n.d.). Annual Report 2024 | GSK. https://www.gsk.com/en-gb/investors/financial-reports/annual-report-2024/

Conversations for tomorrow #6: The CEO Corner - Capgemini UK. (2025, March 10). Capgemini UK. https://www.capgemini.com/gb-en/insights/research-library/conversations-for-tomorrow-6-the-ceo-corner/

Schneider Electric. (2023). Integrated Report: Financial and Sustainable Development. Schneider Electric SA. https://www.se.com/ww/en/assets/564/document/463535/Integrated-report-2023.pdf

Rose Marcario: Environmentalism is for everyone. (2020, January 15). Stanford Graduate School of Business. https://www.gsb.stanford.edu/insights/rose-marcario-environmentalism-everyone

Candelon, F., Krayer, L., & Zhukov, L. (2023, May 25). The CEO's guide to the Generative AI Revolution. BCG Global. https://www.bcg.com/publications/2023/ceo-guide-to-ai-revolution

Spanier, G. (2021, March 19). Sir Martin Sorrell interview: 'S4 Capital's real competition is Accenture' Campaign. https://www.campaignlive.co.uk/article/sir-martin-sorrell-interview-s4-capitals-real-competition-accenture/1699117

Lewis, S. (2025, January 14). Sir Martin Sorrell: 'The role of a CMO has got easier' Campaign. https://www.campaignlive.co.uk/article/sir-martin-sorrell-the-role-cmo-easier/1902174

www.ingramcontent.com/pod-product-compliance
Lightning Source LLC
LaVergne TN
LVHW052314200926
848481LV00002B/560